LEGAL GUIDE

for Day-to-Day Church Matters

A Handbook for
Pastors and
Church Members
Revised and Expanded

CYNTHIA S. MAZUR AND
RONALD K. BULLIS

The Pilgrim Press
Cleveland

To my grandparents,
Mildred and Floyd Bullis and
Leslie and Charlotte Tuttle,
whose lives
help form my own unfolding

RON BULLIS

For Ken, Brenda, and Ruth,
three iridescent lights

CINDY MAZUR

The Pilgrim Press, 700 Prospect Avenue East
Cleveland, Ohio 44115-1100
www.pilgrimpress.com
© 1994, 2003 by Cynthia S. Mazur and Ronald K. Bullis

This book is not intended to replace legal counsel.
Always consult your lawyer.

Biblical quotations are from the *New Revised Standard Version* of the
Bible, © 1989 by the Division of Christian Education of the
National Council of the Churches of Christ in the U.S.A.,
and are used by permission

All rights reserved. Published 1994, 2003

Printed in the United States of America on acid-free paper
07 06 05 04 03   5 4 3 2 1

Library of Congress Cataloging-in-Publication Data
Mazur, Cynthia S., 1954-
    Legal guide for day-to-day church matters : a handbook for pastors
and church members / Cynthia S. Mazur and Ronald K. Bullis.
    —Rev. and expanded
        p.   cm.
    Includes bibliographical references.
    ISBN 0-8298-1555-4 (pbk.)
    1. Ecclesiastical law—United States.   2. Clergy—Legal status, laws,
etc.—United States   3. Church and state—United States.   I. Bullis,
Ronald K.   II. Title.

KF4865.M33   2003
340'.024'2—dc21   2003043383

Contents

LEGAL GUIDE
for Day-to-Day Church Matters

Introduction

MOST PEOPLE, even pastors, administrators, and lay leaders, pay little or no attention to legal issues unless a crisis compels them to do so. It is often assumed that good intentions are enough to ward off legal troubles. Sometimes church professionals believe that the purported separation of church and state immunizes them. Some even may resent the increased intrusion of civil authority into church affairs. Whatever the reason, the continued dismissal of proactive and far-reaching preparation of the church for legal issues continues to cost the church moral authority, the respect of other professionals, and money.

This book has been updated from its first printing in 1989. At that time it was the authors' hope that it would prompt a sustained and serious legal audit by all levels of church government by means of an easily affordable book. The urgency for such a book was clear then; it is even clearer now.

The need to keep current in legal trends is also clear. One of the major innovations in the past couple of years is the introduction of the government's faith-based initiatives. The secular grants to churches and to other nonprofit organizations can make substantial and sustained differences in the lives of the clients and the organization itself.

Obviously this volume cannot hope to address all the legal issues confronted by churches. Nor can it answer specific questions arising from individual circumstances. Those questions are best answered by lawyers familiar with the specific law involved. This book is a primer and a handbook as well as a call to awareness and accountability.

CHAPTER I

Litigation

Ignorantia facri excusar—ignorantia juris non excusat.

Ignorance of fact excuses—ignorance of the law does not excuse.

—R. H. Kersley
Broom's Legal Maxims

JEFF ANDERSON, this country's foremost attorney bringing and winning lawsuits against churches, has stated that churches are very much at risk because they have failed to grasp their legal responsibilities to their parishioners. He also believes that other professions and other institutions are much more sensitive to legal requirements than ministers and churches. To better understand the intricacies of the law and the impact of court decisions, a general background of the court structure is an essential starting point.

How does the court system work?

Litigation begins when a person files a lawsuit or an action in a court of law and encompasses all of the legal proceedings that follow from that point onward. A person brings a legal action asking the court to enforce a right or to remedy a wrong.[1]

America has two court systems: the state court system, which decides and interprets matters of state law, and the federal court system. Matters of federal law or suits involving citizens of different states when the sum in controversy exceeds seventy-five thousand dollars may be brought before a federal court.

The federal court system has three tiers. The federal district court is a trial court with one judge presiding. A case may proceed in the district court with or without a jury. There are over one hundred federal district courts in the country. After losing in the district court, a case may be appealed to the next level, the circuit court of appeals, of which there are thirteen. These courts do not conduct trials. Normally the attorneys for both sides present a twenty-minute argument to a panel of three judges. Several months thereafter the court will issue a formal written decision.

Every case generally has at least one automatic right of appeal. However, the highest court in the land, the Supreme Court, has few cases that it is obligated to hear. Instead, out of roughly five thousand annual requests for review, the Court carefully selects about two hundred. No further avenue of recourse is open if the case is lost before the Supreme Court or if the Supreme Court declines to review the case. Again, an attorney from each side presents a time-limited argument before the nine justices.

A suit brought against a church on the basis of state law such as contract or civil injury will be brought in state court normally. If a church were to bring suit on the basis that the state was interfering with the church's rights to freely practice religion or the state was unfairly establishing religion, these cases would be brought in federal court because they involve constitutional rights.

Do the courts accord religious institutions and religious beliefs any special status?

Yes, the First Amendment of the U.S. Constitution, which is the first article of our Bill of Rights, states, "Congress shall make no law respecting an establishment of religion, or prohibiting the free exercise thereof." The courts and legislatures are bound by this stricture. The government may not promote, restrict, or control religion. When government conduct unduly influences religion one way or the other, there may be a cause of action.

What is charitable immunity?

Desiring to protect churches from exposure to financial liability, states have for many years given churches a freedom from tort suits under the doctrine of "charitable immunity." A tort is a private or civil wrong or injury other than a contract dispute for which the law will allow monetary damages. Generally this wrong involves a violation of a commonly accepted duty.[2]

The doctrine of charitable immunity invalidated tort actions brought by parishioners or others against the church. One of the bases for charitable immunity may well have been the Middle Ages theory that clergy were "civilly dead" and subject only to ecclesiastical laws.[3] American courts adopted the doctrine in the middle of the 1800s, and it has had a checkered and controversial evolution to present day.[4] The scope of charitable immunity extended to churches differs from state to state.

Four theories explain the doctrine of charitable immunity. First, according to the trust-fund theory, funds were thought to be held in trust for the benefit and purposes of the charity.[5] If the court allowed a person harmed by the church to sue the church, the money donated to the church for charitable purposes would be money diverted for unintended purposes. Second, religious employers should not be held responsible for the torts of their employees, as secular employers normally would, because religious employers receive no economic benefit from their employees. Thus it would be unfair to make them financially responsible. Third, charities perform services similar to those provided by the government and as such should enjoy an immunity analogous to sovereign immunity.[6] A final theory involves the idea that immunity promotes and encourages donors to give freely to charities that serve society.[7] Without immunity, the organization's ability to provide good works would be undermined.

In 1942 these undergirding theories were carefully examined by a District of Columbia court and found to be without merit. From that point forward the doctrine began to crumble. Regarding the first theory, the court stated that donors to the church should not be able to immunize their money from liability just by giving it to a charity. Clearly if the donors had kept the money, they would be subject to suit.

Regarding the second theory, it was reasoned that church employers *should* be held responsible for the torts of their employees because they do receive some benefit from them. Additionally, employers are in the best position to protect the public from employee torts. The state should not use its power to nullify the consequences of a church's actions. Indeed it is the state's job to encourage careful selection and training of employees. Moreover, the institution would be in a better position to bear the cost than the individual. This desire to protect the individual is probably the main reason that the immunity doctrine became fraught with exceptions. The courts did not want to allow individuals hurt by the church to bear all of the financial cost of the injury when they were not at fault and had fewer resources than the church.

Regarding the issue of protecting the church's resources, the institution is able to and should procure insurance against these types of problems, just as a profit-making institution does. In fact some states have refused to apply the doctrine of charitable immunity once they determined that the church had insurance.

New exceptions to and applications of the doctrine began to emerge. Some courts have looked at the activity that gave rise to the suit against the church. If the church were having a bazaar or some analogous activity, it was raising money and not engaged in charitable activity. Thus the doctrine would not immunize the church from suit if a person were hurt at the bazaar. Other courts have examined whether the person injured was a beneficiary of the charity. If so, that person had implicitly waived his or her right to sue the charity.

For many people it seemed unfair to deny church members a right to sue when others outside of the church had this right. Some people have argued that if an injured individual could not afford to pay for damages sustained by the acts of a charitable institution, the injured would become the responsibility of the state. The taxpayer would therefore become an unintentional contributor to the charity.

While charitable immunity may be appealing in theory, in practice it can become tantamount to carte blanche, that is, protecting churches that harm others. For instance, New Jersey is one of the few states that has kept its charitable immunity doctrine fully intact. In one case, Coakeley, a Franciscan brother, sexually abused two boys, one thirteen and one eleven, over a period of time and threatened them with harm if they told anyone. The truth came to light and both boys received psychiatric treatment. The youngest was committed to a mental institution and shortly thereafter committed suicide. His mother then had a nervous breakdown. When the parents brought suit against the archdiocese for alleged negligent hiring and supervision, the court dismissed the case without discussion on the basis of charitable immunity.[8]

One commentator has suggested that the public attitude has changed. The desire to protect society's need for strong religious institutions has yielded to ensuring an individual's financial recourse in the event of church-caused trauma.[9] This shift in public perception suggests that society no longer desires to assign a special status to the church. Nonetheless, the viability of churches has not been seriously undermined by the loss of charitable immunity. A church should determine whether charitable immunity exists in its state, determine the scope of the doctrine, and buy insurance accordingly.

What should the church do if it gets sued?

In the not unlikely event that the church is sued, it should find a lawyer who has expertise in the relevant area of the law through the bar referral system (see chap. 16). What follows in this book is meant as a means of prevention only; it is no substitute for specific legal advice or representation. The facts of an individual case combined with the intricacies of the laws of an individual state will have enormous bearing on the posture of the case. In terms of prevention, attorney Jeff Anderson has stated that the best advice is for churches to be candid, responsible, and have clean hands. That is, the church must have done nothing to contribute to the harm.

Is anything to be gained from settling out of court?

In a case in which a church janitor molests a young retarded youth at a dance and loud music and dim lights work to the janitor's advantage, settlement out of court may be preferable. In such a situation, a church sued civilly by parents for poor supervision or negligent hiring might want to reduce publicity that would hurt the church and the victim. Very often the victim would garner a great deal of public sympathy, and the church assumes a moral liability if nothing else. If a church is unable to settle, there is something to be gained by admitting fault to a certain degree. In a recent case against the Catholic Church, the archdiocese admitted that the church was guilty of negligence but stated that it had not willfully employed an unfit priest.

In those instances in which the church faces the question of whether to discipline an employee, to sue an individual, or to turn evidence over to the state prosecutor, issues of forgiveness and redemption will be factors. This of course presents complexities for the church. In one case, a church fired its secretary because the secretary had been involved in serious misconduct. The press wrote an article making the church look like it had treated the secretary most unfairly. The church, however, chose to protect the secretary at its own expense and refused to publicly disclose the reasons for the firing. The church must weigh these complexities. Obviously settling out of court is less desirable when a person or institution wants their reputation exonerated.

Can a church force parties to mediate?

The church may place mediation clauses in its written agreements. Thus when the church enters into contracts, it can include the parties' agreement to mediate civil suits. The church can always encourage mediation as a quick, private, and more satisfying way to resolve disputes.

The church or the pastor can *encourage* people in general to mediate their differences instead of pursuing litigation. The local court system may have a mandatory mediation program, and private mediation services can be located in the phone book. Additionally, the state bar association will have helpful information on alternative dispute resolution.

Can the church sue?

The church can file a lawsuit and of course it should vigorously defend itself against suit if settlement is not preferred. If a church were to determine that it was being harassed by federal or state actions, it may want to react aggressively. The church should be particularly sensitive when laws burden it more heavily than other churches or secular institutions.

Should the church have a lawyer on retainer?

Unless the church is very large with many property holdings or commercial operations, retaining a lawyer is not necessary. However, churches should routinely seek a lawyer's advice as a means of *avoiding* legal trouble.

Does the church have to reveal its records to the government or to the court?

The Church Audit Procedures Act (CAPA) of the 1984 Tax Reform Act provides that before the IRS may begin an inquiry into the tax status of any organization claiming to be a church, the IRS must satisfy certain prerequisites. Among other things it must articulate a reasonable belief in the need for an investigation and provide special notice to the church.[10] Further, the statute circumscribes the scope of examinations, allowing the IRS to demand documents only "to the extent necessary" to determine tax liability or tax-exempt status.[11] Records that would trace the flow of funds within the church or discover the identity of sources of income probably would not be reviewable. Records that would shed light on possible commercial purposes, for example, documents detailing the goods and services offered by the church, how they are priced, and to whom they are provided, would be reviewable. Moreover, the IRS could obtain documents to track all funds leaving the organization to expose methods of removing profits.[12]

Incidentally, a state has no authority to know a person's membership in or support of any church. The state may not inquire what a person believes, how he or she practices religion, or how he or she supports religious activities. The state may issue a properly narrow summons to investigate whether the church is operating within the limited purposes for which it was incorporated and therefore can properly retain its nonprofit status.

Is the church building a real sanctuary from the law?

Church buildings are not actual sanctuaries from the law, but few prosecutors or police officers would welcome the direct conflict that forcibly entering a church would entail. The ancient Phoenicians, Syrians, Egyptians, and Greeks recognized the concept that a church could be a safe haven from the law.[13] Sanctuary emerged as a result of the harsh system of retributive justice that existed at the beginning of Western Civilization. The Bible named sanctuary cities to which accidental murderers could flee.[14] Once there, the murderer was protected from acts of retribution. The biblical tradition became part of Roman law with the rise of the Christian state in the fourth century.[15]

Sanctuary was part of the English common law, was codified in canon law during the Middle Ages, and was eventually incorporated into European civil law.[16] Its use declined under Henry VIII after he required those who availed themselves of its benefits to be branded.[17] By the eighteenth century, sanctuary had fallen into disuse and was looked upon as a "vestige of Romanism and popery."[18]

In America sanctuary has been invoked to help slaves who were trying to escape, AWOL soldiers, and Central American refugees.[19] The closest thing that the American judicial system has to sanctuary is the doctrine of separation of church and state. Thus from time to time a court will rule that a criminal matter is off limits to the court because of a First Amendment exemption for churches. Recently in Chicago a state judge ruled that the Roman Catholic archdiocese would not be required to reveal certain communications about priests accused of child sexual abuse. The church argued that the material should remain confidential, and the court agreed.[20] Generally courts are less and less inclined to allow for sanctuary in criminal matters.

Does the government have the right to infiltrate the church as a member to gather information?

In 1984, the Immigration and Naturalization Service (INS) initiated an undercover investigation of the sanctuary movement. INS agents infiltrated and surreptitiously recorded several services and collected license plate numbers of members in four churches in Arizona. The churches alleged that as a result membership participation declined, a Bible-study group had to be canceled because of lack of participation, financial support decreased, pastoral time was diverted, congregants became reluctant to seek counseling, and congregants were less open in prayers and confessions. As such, the court determined that a church could sue the government if its illegal activity deterred church adherents from freely participating in religious activities protected by the First Amendment. The government may not illegally interfere with the church's ability to carry out its mission.[21]

CHAPTER 2

Church Procedures

Dies dominicus non est juridicus.
Sunday is not a day for judicial or legal proceedings.
—R. H. Kersley
Broom's Legal Maxims

T HE LEGAL MAXIM ABOVE indicates that the wheels of justice cease on Sunday out of respect for religion. Rarely, however, does the church take similar account of the law, particularly in its own operations. The church is a legal entity that can sue and be sued and is subject to limited control by state and federal law. The court will accord church action legal recognition if the church has taken its procedures seriously. Formalizing, clarifying, documenting adherence to, and when necessary, amending church procedures are very important measures.

Many church suits involve a fight for leadership and focus on the question of who was the rightful owner of the property when the church split. Church procedures become particularly important during such church schisms and property disputes. For instance, Reverend White of Houston's First Missionary Baptist Church was sued because he refused to abide by a church election to dismiss him.[1] The election results were twenty-four votes to fire him and twenty-three votes to retain him. White responded to the vote by changing the locks on the church doors and continuing to preach. The majority sought a court order to force White to leave and to assess ten thousand dollars in damages against him, because the dispute resulted in lost attendance and financial support. White asserted that the election was not valid. Moreover, he stated that he had founded the church seven years prior and was the owner of the property. The outcome of this case will turn on whether the proper church procedures were followed for the election.

Do church procedures need to be written down?

Yes, church procedures need to be formalized in writing. Normally the church sets forth its basic organizing rules in the church constitution or bylaws. These rules will control all church activity and will define the functions and powers of each committee and the rights and obligations of the officers. The document will contain, for example, the rules regarding how to call a meeting. Assuming this document conforms to state law regarding charitable organizations, any action taken that is contrary to the formal bylaws is voidable if challenged. It is important for the church to define in this document who is allowed to vote on church matters, what constitutes a quorum, and when unanimity is required as opposed to a simple majority of those present. The courts will rely on these documents as the first point of reference in church disputes over property, church polity, and church administration.

Do minutes of meetings need to be taken?

Minutes will become critical for many legal issues related to trustee, deacon, or council liability. Minutes authorize church business and the conduct of the church's agents in pursuit of its business. Minutes establish whether one has been given authority to purchase a computer, enter into a contract, or fire an employee. If such authority has properly been assigned according to the bylaws or constitution, then the minutes establish whether a person has exercised that authority in conformity with the church's instructions.

Many board members want to know whether they are liable for church debts. A governing officer has no personal liability if he or she is specifically authorized by the proper governing body to purchase a church van, for example. Such authorization would normally be determined from meeting minutes. Without authority this person can be held personally liable for debts he or she incurs on behalf of the church. Additionally, the board responsible and liable for church activities must always act in the best interest of the church. Board members should be very cautious about any act that would give the appearance of self-dealing.

Does adherence to church procedures have any legal significance?

If a church fails to follow its own rules regarding, for example, the calling of a special meeting or what constitutes a voting member, the action in question will be null and void as far as the court is concerned.

Does the church need to define what constitutes a bona fide member and keep a current roster?

Yes, the church does need to define a member and keep a current roster. In one recent case where a church split into two factions, the question of who was a voting member became critical. One part of the church wanted to break away and take the church building with it. The court determined that a prior vote had not been conducted properly. The vote legally recognized by the court would determine which group would retain control of the church. The church's bylaws indicated that the vote would be won by a majority, that any member could vote, and that a member remained a member "until death or dismissal." One faction went through all of the old membership records and contacted numerous people who had moved or were away at school. These people returned in large numbers for the vote and greatly affected the election. The court ruled that as long as the church procedures were adhered to, the election was legal and binding.

In a very different case a dispute arose over a person's desire to remain a member when the rest of the church had decided to terminate her membership. The former member requested a court order reinstating her membership and damages totaling fifty thousand dollars. She alleged that the church intentionally inflicted emotional distress on her by terminating her "lifelong" membership after she assisted a former pastor in finding new employment. Apparently this assistance placed her membership status in doubt. Reviewing the church's documents regarding membership, the court refused to substitute its judgment for the church's. It would not second-guess the tenet that members were expected, first of all, "to be faithful in all the duties essential to the Christian life."[2]

Does the church need to set forth the duties of the various jobs in the church such as deacon, elder, or trustee?

Yes, it is only with clear delineation that church officers will know their duties, obligations, and the powers bestowed on them by the church. Needless to say, the parameters of a board member's powers and authority should not be exceeded nor capriciously changed. Bylaws must be amended in accordance with normal church procedures. As mentioned above, the church officers responsible for the church are under a legal obligation to act in the best interest of the church. They should avoid even the appearance of impropriety.

In New York State, the parents of sexually abused minors brought a suit against the minister, the perpetrator; the True Church of God, which was registered as a religious corporation; its various trustees and officers; and several related entities. Under the bylaws of the church, the minister had nearly absolute authority over the church, its trustees, officers, members, and related churches. The court determined that the church officers could not assert immunity unless they could show that there was no gross negligence or intentional harm on their part. If these people blindly followed the orders of the minister and did not act in the best interest of the church, the court stated that they could be held liable for proceeding in reckless disregard of the consequences of their acts. Additionally, the defendants would have to offer an affidavit of the chief financial officer of the corporation attesting to the corporation's nonprofit status.[3] State law sets forth the exact parameters of liability to which board members are exposed. Every state has its own nuances just as every church constitution does.

How does the church draft a proper motion?

A proper motion should be short but include thorough answers to the questions of who, what, where, when, and how. The motion should state which body of the church has drafted it and in response to what circumstances. It should state plainly when the motion will come for a vote and who will be voting on it. If for instance the church council is making a motion to form a new committee, then this new committee's duties should be specifically designated, the expected duration of the committee's tenure should be stated, and the members or procedure for selection of the members should be specified. Eventualities should be planned for, such as vacancies, how often the committee will meet, whom the board will report to, and the form of the final product if the committee is created for a specific task. The motion should also state the powers that it does not confer, such as the power to spend money or enter into contracts.

CHAPTER 3

Government Regulatory Laws

Salus populi est suprema lex.
Regard for the public welfare is the highest law.
—R. H. Kersley
Broom's Legal Maxims

ALTHOUGH PROTECTING the public welfare may be the highest goal of state law, sometimes churches argue that such laws impose undue burdens on their activities. One of the duties placed on the state is to protect the public health, morals, and welfare. At the same time the government is prohibited by the Constitution from interfering with the free exercise of religion. The government then is in the difficult position of balancing its duty to allow religious activity with its duty to protect the public welfare. Accordingly, religious institutions will sometimes be exempted or request exemptions from certain laws that limit the free exercise of religion. For instance, a church sued a hospital accreditation association, requesting the court to exempt its religious hospital from obstetrics-gynecology residency program requirements that provided clinical training in family planning procedures.[1] The court had to balance its duty to protect the public health with its duty to protect the church from state regulation. It decided that a religious exemption was not in order.

In 1990 the Supreme Court decided the pivotal case of *Employment Div., Dep't of Human Resources v. Smith*, denying free exercise exemptions when they involve neutral laws of general applicability.[2] In *Smith* two rehabilitation counselors were dismissed from their jobs and denied unemployment compensation because they admitted to ingesting peyote during a religious ceremony of the Native American Church of which they were members. The counselors argued that they had been dismissed unfairly and were prohibited from practicing their religion. The Court stated that the First Amendment will not shield criminal behavior from prosecution when the laws in question are religiously neutral and apply to everyone. Immediately thereafter, a coalition of religious groups constructed a legislative override to the Court's decision. In 1993 President Clinton signed the Religious Freedom Restoration Act, which mandated that a state or the Federal government would have to demonstrate a compelling interest to substantially burden an individual's free exercise of religion.

How have historic preservation laws impacted churches?

Recently historic-preservation laws have had serious economic ramifications for churches. Historic-preservation laws grow out of the state's zoning powers. The state's ability to control land use flows from the state's strongest interest: the use of its broad police powers to preserve the health, safety, and welfare of society as a whole. The church of course wants to conduct its activities free from the state's control.

In a recent case a federal appellate court found that the designation of a church as historic and the concomitant inability to make changes to its property did not violate the church's free exercise rights.[3] The Episcopal church even requested that the buildings be decertified as landmarks but to no avail.

St. Bartholomew's landmark designation prohibited the alteration or demolition of its buildings without approval by the Landmarks Preservation Committee of New York City. In

1983 the church requested that it be allowed to replace the Community House with a fifty-nine-story office tower. St. Bartholomew's Community House was adjacent to the church and was the center for a variety of social and religious activities. The court ruled that there was no improper taking of the property without just compensation on the part of the state, because the church was not so severely restricted in its ability to use its property. The historic-preservation law did not prevent the church from continuing current charitable and religious activities, even if the landmark designation froze the church's property in its existing use and prevented expansion. Any deprivation of commercial value was not an unlawful state-taking without just compensation as long as continued use for present activities was viable.

The court acknowledged that the church would suffer from a reduced income if it were forced to repair instead of replace the Community House. The church, however, failed to show that its budget could not withstand this diminution.[4] The church stated that it was in the unfair position of having to seek secular approval for a decision on how to use its resources. Needless to say the church asserted that it had a constitutional right not to have its conduct hindered by landmark laws. The court disagreed. Shortly thereafter the St. Paul and St. Andrew United Methodist Church filed a suit against the New York Landmarks Commission for thirty million dollars in alleged damages suffered as a result of its landmark designation.[5] The church has not prevailed.

Are there other instances in which the zoning power may affect the activities of the religious organization?

To date, zoning laws have been challenged either because they give too much power to local churches or because they unreasonably inhibit the conduct of churches as in the St.

Bartholomew case mentioned above. In 2000 Congress enacted the Religious Land Use and Institutionalized Persons Act,[6] which prohibits zoning and other land use authorities from discriminating against or unnecessarily burdening the religious practices of religious institutions or places of worship, including the ability to provide social ministries.[7]

It has been difficult to draw the appropriate line between church independence and state authority to zone. In one case it was determined that the state had given the church too much power over the state's zoning authority. In *Larkin v. Grendel's Den, Inc.*,[8] Massachusetts passed a statute that provided that any church could prevent an applicant from obtaining a liquor license if the applicant's business was to be located within five hundred feet of a church. Churches were in effect given complete veto power over some of the most commercially valuable sites. A restaurant owner challenged the law. The Supreme Court concluded that the primary and principal effect of the statute was to advance religion, a purpose prohibited by the First Amendment, and accordingly ruled that the statute was unconstitutional. How religious property fits into the state and local zoning schemes is a very important piece of information for the local church, synagogue, or mosque.

Do churches, mosques, and synagogues have to abide by charitable-solicitation ordinances?

States and cities have been known to regulate religious organizations through charitable-solicitation ordinances.[9] In *Larson v. Valente* (1982) religious denominations in Minnesota receiving more than 50 percent of their funds from members and affiliated organizations were not required to comply with registration and reporting laws regarding their fundraising activities. This statute had the effect of granting a denominational preference to well-established churches. Minnesota explained that it had a compelling state interest in protecting its citizens from abusive solicitation practices. The Supreme Court determined that the law favored one religion over another and extended the exemption to the Unification Church of Sun Myung Moon. Following the Supreme Court's signal, a Fort Lauderdale court struck down a similar charitable-solicitation ordinance as unconstitutional because it regulated churches that did not have permanent edifices.[10]

Recently a U.S. Court of Appeals held that solicitation of funds by religious organizations is protected religious-expressive activity under the First Amendment.[11] Indeed the court questioned whether the solicitation ordinance in issue had been passed solely to discriminate against the Church of Scientology, for it appeared from the legislative record that there had been a movement "intent on driving Scientology from Clearwater."

Clearwater, a city in Florida, passed an ordinance imposing substantial record keeping and disclosure requirements on all charities and religious organizations soliciting funds in Clearwater. If an organization solicited without obtaining a registration certificate, it would be subject to criminal penalties, including jail sentences and fines. The ordinance committed investigation and enforcement activities to the prosecutorial and judicial authorities.

The court found that the ordinance violated the First Amendment because it required excessive entanglement between the church and the local government. The ordinance called for detailed monitoring and close administrative interaction between the church and the city. The religious organization had to disclose the *purpose* for which funds would be and had been solicited and the uses to which funds would be and had been put. The entire functioning of the church would become a matter of public record. The ordinance also required disclosure of the amount of funds spent on salaries, overhead and the like, and the names and addresses of every person in the organization with authority to spend its money. If funds were to be spent elsewhere in the world, the ordinance required disclosure of church activity worldwide. Thus the court invalidated, for purposes of religious organizations only, many provisions of the statute that required excessive interaction between the church and state.

The court also reviewed one part of the ordinance that required the soliciting organization to provide a written statement of the terms and conditions upon which refunds would be made. The city had a legitimate interest in preventing deception, manipulation, and coercion. And it is well settled that one may not willfully and fraudulently omit material facts in the course of attempting to secure money from others. Thus the court found that this requirement did not violate the First Amendment and placed no unfair burden on the religious organization soliciting funds.

In conclusion, churches, mosques, and synagogues do have to abide by normal charitable solicitation ordinances. The government has a legitimate interest in protecting the public from fraud and harassment. If a particular church, however, finds that an ordinance is unfair to it or unduly burdensome, it should assert its rights.

Does a church-run day-care center need to comply with state licensing requirements?

Each state handles religious day-care exemptions differently. Most states require day-care centers to obtain a license and comply with certain basic health standards. Licensing requirements ordinarily relate to issues of space, health, nutrition, disciplinary practices, and parental participation. In Virginia some churches informed state authorities that their religious beliefs would not permit them to apply for or accept a state license to carry out a function they considered an integral part of their religious ministry. The Virginia legislature enacted a law exempting religious day-care centers from licensing requirements.[12] Secular child-care centers brought suit, asserting that the state was favoring and promoting religion, because the law gave religious day-care centers a competitive advantage.

Under the First Amendment of the U.S. Constitution, the government may not interfere with one's right to freely exercise his or her religion. Additionally, the government may not establish religion. Thus the government is prohibited from supporting religion or giving it preferential treatment. Part of this prohibition includes a mandate that the government must not involve itself in church affairs. A federal appeals court decided that the religious exemption was valid and stated that the state had simply adopted a hands-off policy consistent with the separation of church and state doctrine.

Does a youth camp or other religious operation need to comply with state licensing requirements?

In Oklahoma the courts have found that the duty to protect public welfare outweighs the duty to allow freedom of worship.[13] The Calvary Baptist Church refused to obtain the required license to operate its Calvary Boys Ranch. The law in question required that the facility provide: (1) a constructive program and services to meet the needs of each child and family; (2) staff of good moral character and ability for child care; (3) adequate and safe housekeeping, sanitation, and equipment; (4) good health care and full educational and religious opportunities; (5) good community relationships; (6) essential records and administrative methods; and (7) sufficient funds for sound operation. The operators stated that the requirements violated their free exercise rights. The court disagreed, stating that the state had the duty to protect its minor citizens. The court was particularly concerned where young children were completely controlled by and entirely dependent on child-care operators and employees for all of their needs.

Similarly, the Salvation Army requested that it be allowed to disregard highly detailed and lengthy zoning laws related to boarding homes for purposes of its group home establishments.[14] The court decided that the boardinghouse statutes applied to everyone and were not specifically directed at prohibiting religious practices. The court balanced the competing interests in favor of public health. As such, the Salvation Army's free exercise claim failed.

Does a church-run soup kitchen need to comply with the state health or nuisance laws?

Yes, a church-run soup kitchen must comply with state health laws; however, even if the church conducts its activities in a perfectly lawful manner, the state may still interfere with its operations. In 1982 Episcopal Community Services in Arizona opened a center for indigent food distribution in a residential area.[15] A neighborhood association brought suit to stop the program, alleging that it constituted a public nuisance. The association alleged that transients were drawn to the area and remained there at length, urinating, defecating, and drinking on the residents' properties. The parties agreed that the center had not violated any zoning or criminal law. The court decided that the church's lawful operation could be prohibited for acts committed off of the church's premises by clients no longer under the church's direction or control. The church could be held responsible for its patrons, because the church frequently attracted these clients to the area.

Must the church comply with the Americans with Disabilities Act?

The Americans with Disabilities Act (ADA) of 1990 specifically exempts churches from its purview. Religious organizations, entities controlled by religious organizations, and places of worship do not have to physically reconstruct their operations to make their facilities more accessible to the handicapped.

The ADA's religious exemption is very broad.[16] Even when a religious organization carries out activities that would otherwise make it a public entity, the religious organization is exempt. If a church itself operates a day-care center, nursing home, private school, or diocesan school system, the operations would not be subject to the ADA. The religious entity would not lose its exemption merely because the services provided were open to the general public. The test is whether the church or other religious organization operates the activity, not who receives the services.[17]

Entities that are controlled by religious organizations are exempt from the ADA. If the religious organization uses a lay board or other secular or corporate mechanism to operate schools or an array of social services, the exemption still applies. The test remains a factual one: whether the church or other religious organization controls the operations of the school or service or whether the school or service is itself a religious organization.[18]

A public entity that is not itself a religious organization but operates a place of public accommodation in leased space on the property of a religious entity, which is not a place of worship, is subject to the ADA's requirements if it is not under control of a religious organization. When a church rents meeting space, which is not a place of worship, to a local community group or to a private, independent day-care center, the ADA applies to the activities of the local group and day-care center if a lease exists and payment is required as part of the lease.[19]

Although churches are exempt, most churches that will comply with this law will do so not because they must but because they believe that it is right for their membership. It will be the responsibility of the local church along with representatives of the disabled community to identify what changes are necessary and to set priorities.

Must the church comply with the Fair Housing Act?

The Fair Housing Act requires nondiscrimination and fair housing throughout the United States,[20] but it does not apply to any religious organization, association, society, or any nonprofit institution or organization operated, supervised, or controlled by or in conjunction with a religious organization, association, or society. Thus the religious organization may, without fear of violating the law, limit the sale, rental, or occupancy of dwellings that it owns or operates for other than a commercial purpose to persons of the same religion. The organization may give preference to such persons unless membership in the religion is restricted on the basis of race, color, or national origin.[21] This provision becomes important particularly for denominational retirement homes.

Can churches offer religious instruction, Bible study, and prayer and hymn sings in a public school?

Yes, if the school is open to other organizations for public-welfare meetings after hours, a church cannot be excluded from access on the basis that the club is religious in nature. These meetings must be open to the general public and not be sponsored by the school.[22]

CHAPTER 4

Faith-based Initiatives

Nemo debet esse judex in propria sua causa.
No man can be judge in his own cause.

—R. H. Kersley
Broom's Legal Maxims

DOES THE CHURCH SHOW its bias in either supporting or opposing the president's Faith-based Initiatives? There appears to be substantial controversy as to whether these initiatives will help or harm the church. President Bush stated when he created his Armies of Compassion agenda at the beginning of 2001, "The Federal Government will play a new role as supporter, enabler, catalyst and collaborator with faith-based and community organizations." The president wants to promote faith-based organizations because they "serve people in need, not just by providing services but also by transforming lives."

What is meant by the president's Armies of Compassion agenda?

In January of 2001 President Bush announced his initiative to strengthen faith and community-based organizations. He calls these organizations, "the armies of compassion that labor daily to strengthen families and communities." By signing two executive orders, he created a new White House Office called Faith-based and Community Initiatives. The president directed five cabinet agencies each to create a Center for Faith-based and Community Initiatives. These include the departments of Health and Human Services, Housing and Urban Development, Labor, Justice, and Education. The president's agenda significantly broadens the scope and extent of government financial collaboration with faith-based organizations. In December 2002 President Bush signed two executive orders that moved the faith-based initiatives forward. Together, they affirmed the intent of faith-based initiatives and authorized specific steps toward wide implementation. They also authorized "Centers" within the Department of Agriculture and the Agency for International Development, among other things, to examine and eliminate unfair barriers to faith groups receiving government funds when they apply for grants and to disseminate information to potential grantees.

The president's agenda includes the Charity Aid, Recovery, and Empowerment Act (CARE Act, which as drafted in May 2002 encourages charitable giving through tax incentives; provides up to 33 million dollars to support certain vulnerable populations, such as teenage unwed mothers; provides 275 million dollars for the Social Service Block Grant that supports organizations such as Meals on Wheels; creates a Compassion Capital Fund of 150 million dollars to fund technical assistance to help small community and faith-based charities increase capacity, improve competence, and expand programs. Additionally, these funds will provide start-up capital to smaller groups to expand or emulate model programs. The act creates a 501(c)(3) EZ Pass process to help faith-based organizations get tax-deductible status more easily. The EZ Pass process relaxes the definition of faith-based organizations to include nonprofit corporations with a religious affiliation. The CARE Act increases access of faith-based charities to federal funds by prohibiting discrimination against organizations based on religious grounds.

What are faith-based initiatives?

Faith-based initiatives involve federal or state legislation under which churches and other faith-based groups can become partners with government agencies. Faith groups receive grants to help the homeless, provide food and clothing, and to help the less fortunate. As such, the Salvation Army, Catholic Charities, and Jewish Social Services receive federal or state money to provide services to those in need.

The president states that the goal of his faith-based initiatives is to strengthen, empower, uplift, enlist, and equip the country's faith-based service providers. In addition, he expects to mobilize public support for charitable organizations through volunteerism, public-private partnerships, and increased financial giving.

What is Charitable Choice?

In 1996 Congress passed the Personal Responsibility and Work Opportunity Reconciliation Act (PRWORA), which was signed by the president. This law, part of the overall welfare reform laws passed both by the states and the federal government, gave block grants to states to provide social services.

The Charitable Choice Provision, section 104 of PRWORA, states that religious and charitable organizations should not be discriminated against as grantees that provide social services. This law seeks to "level the playing field" for religious groups to apply for and to receive government grants for social services, such as literacy training, job skills, parenting skills, building or repairing low-income housing, or mentoring. This law had the effect of drawing attention to the partnership between religious groups and government-sponsored programs.

When President George W. Bush was governor of Texas, he found that the PRWORA worked well in his state. Therefore during the 2000 presidential campaign he emphasized the value of faith-based initiatives. Meanwhile many states have duplicated the PRWORA to further emphasize and encourage religious organizations to be treated equally regarding how they are judged in the grant-application process.

First Amendment guarantees about the free exercise of religion are addressed in section 401(d) of the PRWORA. In essence it states that a religious organization with a grant or that accepts certificates, vouchers, or other forms of disbursement shall retain its independence from federal, state, and local governments, including such organization's control over the definition, development, practice, and expression of its religious beliefs. Moreover, the PRWORA states that neither the federal nor the state government can require a group to change its internal governance or to remove religious icons, scriptures, and other symbols.

How did Charitable Choice get started?

Former Senator John Ashcroft (R., Mo.) worked with others from his state to give religious organizations a greater role in receiving government funds. Senator Ashcroft was instrumental in adding Charitable Choice to the 1996 Welfare Reform Act.

Doesn't the U.S. Constitution prohibit government funds flowing to religious groups?

Instead of a "separation" between religion and state, it is now more accurate to speak of "neutrality" and "non-coercion" to describe permissible aid that passes from government to a religious group. In *Rosenberger v. Rector and Visitors of the Univ. of Virginia* (1995), the U.S. Supreme Court permitted a public university to give money to a student group to start a religious newspaper. The Court allowed the university to fund the religious publication because all student groups at the university were treated in a *neutral* manner.

What is likely to occur?

The Care Act is likely to pass in some form. Its large funding goals will probably be downsized. The act is popular because it replaces HR7, which as proposed allowed churches to disregard civil rights laws in their employment practices. Additionally, HR7 allowed churches to display religious symbols and discuss religious issues and concepts as long as the client had access to secular providers.

What are the obligations of a faith-based group when awarded a government contract?

Obligations on the part of the grant-recipient religious organization are designed to protect the taxpayer, the integrity of the grant-making process, and the clients of the grant. If the grant is approved, the religious group must adhere to the specific rules of the grant like any other recipient. The following are principal concepts incumbent on a grant recipient, including a religious grant recipient:

1. Grant recipients must not discriminate against those they are obliged to serve. They must not discriminate against anyone on account of their race, color, gender, creed, national origin, or abilities.

2. Grant recipients cannot use any funds for religious purposes, specifically worship, religious instruction, or evangelism. The religious group may offer services out of religious motivation, but it cannot make religious observance on the part of clients a requirement for receiving services.

Some religious organizations create entirely separate legal entities in order to separate their Charitable Choice from their main organization. For example, a church may create a separate nonprofit organization to run its homeless shelter. These sub-organizations are separate legal entities and serve to preserve the integrity of the government funds from the funds collected by the religious organization for sectarian purposes.

This separation of the sectarian mission from the grant function can have an additional benefit. The sub-organization can provide a legal insulation to the main organization in the event of a civil suit. Let's say a volunteer for the homeless shelter for a church slips and falls while ladling out food. Because the shelter is now a separate legal group, the volunteer might successfully sue the homeless shelter but not the main church. The church funds would remain intact, and the only assets at risk would be the nonprofit homeless shelter.

How do you begin to form a nonprofit organization as mentioned above?

The Internal Revenue Service defines the tax exempt 501(c)(3) status as a group organized and operated exclusively for religious, charitable, scientific, testing for public safety, literary, educational purposes, and that:

1. No part of the net earnings inures to the benefit of any private shareholder or individual.
2. No substantial part of the activities is carrying on propaganda or otherwise attempting to influence legislation (unless as otherwise allowed).
3. Does not participate in or intervene in any political campaign for any candidate.

A group considering forming a nonprofit organization can get help from an attorney in a number of ways. First, private attorneys may be willing to file the necessary paperwork on a pro bono ("for the public good") basis. This means they may do it for free. Second, one may know an attorney who is working for a local 501(c)(3) organization who may be willing to file for the church. Third, local bar associations (lawyers' professional groups) may be willing to file the paper on the church's behalf. A group considering nonprofit status with the IRS should ask for legal and technical help from lawyers and those professionals already involved in 501(c)(3) organizations.

Information on community and faith-based initiatives

Center for Public Justice	cpjustice.org
Welfare Information Network	welfareinfo.org/faithbase.htm
"Faith-based Initiatives and Charitable Choices 2001"	pcusa.org
"Finding Common Ground"	working-group.org
"Keeping the Faith: The Promise of Cooperation, the Perils of Government Funding: A Guide for Houses of Worship"	ucc.org/justice/cc/index.html
Grant Writing The Grants Connection, Inc. 8522 Ben Nevis Dr Richmond VA 23235 804.320.2911	www.grantsconnection.com
The Foundation Center	www.fdncenter.org

CHAPTER 5

Copyright

Qui prior est tempore porior est jure.
He has the better title who was first in point
of time.

—R. H. Kersley
Broom's Legal Maxims

ILLUSTRATING THE LEGAL MAXIM cited above is the following hypothetical. Pastor Smith preaches a Thanksgiving sermon that touches everyone in the congregation. Praise of his sermon reaches several of Smith's colleagues, and they request audiotapes of it. One year later at a Thanksgiving service in a nearby town Pastor Smith hears his sermon delivered by his colleague.

According to *Webster's*, copyright, the protection of intellectual property, is "the exclusive legal right to reproduce, publish, and sell the matter and form of a literary, musical, or artistic work."[1] Smith and his colleagues need to understand the law of copyright for two reasons. The first reason is to avoid violating copyright law by illegally using others' created works. Religious institutions and clergy can easily violate the copyright laws (infringement) in a host of ways. Duplicating choir music, using cartoons and stories for church bulletins and newsletters, writing articles, reproducing sermons, and copying liturgies all pose a copyright infringement danger.

Second, religious organizations and religious professionals need to know how to protect their creative works. Many clergy or religious institutions produce copyrightable material. Religious professionals create sermons, plays, liturgies, articles, and other original words but do not know how to copyright their material or how to protect and prosecute their rights under copyright law. The balance of this chapter describes what is copyrightable, how that is accomplished, what constitutes copyright infringement, and the penalties for infringement.

The English copyright law, out of which American copyright law grew, began in 1556 to stem the spread of the Protestant Reformation. A company comprised of the dominant London publishers was given a publishing monopoly by the Star Chamber—a legal body functioning on behalf of the church and the government. The publishing company censored and suppressed any ideas contrary to the established church.[2]

Modern American law now protects the ownership rights of authors and publishers regarding their original ideas. This protection includes the owner's right to reproduce the work, to prepare derivative works (editions and compilations), to distribute the work, to perform the work, and to display the work. The length of a valid copyright depends on when the work was created. Works made prior to January 1, 1978, are protected for one term of twenty-eight years and a renewable term of another twenty-eight years. Works made after this date are protected longer—for the author's life plus an additional term of seventy years. Once copyright protection is exhausted, works are referred to as being in the "public domain." If a work is in the public domain, the work is no longer protected by copyright and can be reproduced without violating copyright law. Checking with the following organizations can help to determine whether a copyright exists on a certain work:

Copyright Office Library of Congress
Room 401
101 Independence Avenue SE
Washington DC 20559
202.707.3000
202.707.9100 (forms hotline)

Motion Picture Licensing Corporation
1177 Summer St
Stamford CT 06905-0838

Church Music Publishers
Box 158992
Nashville TN 37215

The 1976 Copyright Act establishes what can be copyrighted, how it can be copyrighted, and how copyright infringement occurs. Additionally the United States has joined two global, multilateral copyright treaties—the Universal Copyright Convention and the Berne Convention for the Protection of Literary and Artistic Works. These international treaties offer international copyright protection to U.S. authors in the countries that have ratified these agreements.

What do clergy and other religious professionals produce that is copyrightable?

Almost anything that clergy, religious educators, and other religious professionals create can be copyrighted. The Copyright Act specifies that writing, music, drama, pictures, sculptures, movies, and sound recordings are all acceptable subject matter for copyright protection. Thus written, taped, or otherwise recorded articles, sermons, speeches, presentations, books, musical scores for plays and choirs, liturgical choreography, drama productions, and artwork produced for the bulletin, newsletters, or other such materials are all suitable copyright materials.

There are two legal requirements for works to be eligible for copyright protection: the works must be original, and they must be in a *tangible* form, that is, they cannot be mere ideas.

How can religious professionals proceed with copyrighting their material?

According to the law any tangible, original work created after January 1, 1978, is *already copyrighted*. Copyright protection is simultaneously created when the work itself is created. The work should contain, however, notice of the author's desire to copyright it for purposes of litigation. Moreover, to prosecute a claim of *infringement* in U.S. works, American law requires that the creative work be *registered* with the Copyright Office in Washington, D.C. Even though a work is theoretically protected, once the original work is created in tangible form, creators should use the insignia of notice to copyright.

The notice insignia can be satisfied when the creator places three symbols in this order on the tangible work: the word "copyright" or the copyright symbol ©, the date of creation, and the creator's name. Thus, a copyright insignia placed on a sermon by Reverend Bullis might look like this: "© 2003 Bullis." The insignia should be prominently displayed on the published work an author wants to protect. To protect against inadvertent publication without proper notice of unpublished works, the following formula is used: "Unpublished work © 2003 Bullis."

As mentioned above, under American law, registration is a prerequisite for commencing an infringement action. Works can be registered with the U.S. Copyright Office at the following address:

Registrar of Copyrights
Library of Congress
Room 401
101 Independence Ave SE
Washington DC 20559
202.707.3000
202.707.9100 (forms hotline)

Copyright registration requires an application fee, a thirty-dollar processing fee, and copies of the work to be registered. The Copyright Office receives about 500,000 copyright applications annually.

Under what circumstances can copyrighted material be duplicated and used?

The Copyright Act provides for a "fair use" exception to copyright protection. There are four factors that courts will consider in determining whether the exception applies:[3]

1. *Whether the use is for educational or for commercial purposes.* The "character and purpose" of a work will be evaluated by the court. This element means that the use must have a "transformative" purpose—that is, the copying must change the original matter into something new and different.[4] Merely duplicating others' material is unlikely to meet this test—and courts are likely to consider mere nontransformative duplicating as a factor favoring the author.

2. *The nature of copyrighted work.* The court will review the "nature" of the copyrighted work to determine whether the work is factual or nonfactual. Factual matter (biographies, reviews, or factual criticism) is considered to have great public value and thus require freer public use. For example, if a

religious institution creates a factual work such as a review of the play *Jesus Christ Superstar*, the church is less protected under copyright law than if it created an original religious drama. By the same token, a church that duplicates an original play without permission is more likely to get into copyright trouble than if it duplicates a biography of Martin Luther.

3. *The amount of material used relative to the entire work.* The court will consider how much material is being duplicated. The "amount and substantability" factor cannot be determined with precision. Courts generally agree that copying a small amount of an extremely important part of a work is just as damaging as copying larger portions of less important material. For example, a court held that while the defendant had only copied between 5.2 percent and 25.1 percent of the author's work, the duplicated portions constituted critical sections of the work.[5]

   Another court tried to clarify how much "similarity" is necessary to try a case and to find infringement. It replaced the usual term of "substantial similarity" with a two-part analysis. First, the aggrieved party must show that the defendant has access to the work and/or that there were similarities to the allegedly copied work. This is called "probative similarities." After the plaintiff has proved copying, he or she must show a "substantial similarity" between the works.[6]

4. *The economic impact on the copyrighted material.* The court will assess the economic impact of the duplication. While courts want to ensure public use of creative ideas, the "fair use" exemption is strictly applied to protect the financial interests of creators and publishers. The court will determine whether and to what extent the alleged infringement is likely to interfere with the economic incentives of the publisher or author to continue publishing. The stated policy

of copyright law is to protect the free flow of creative work. To the extent that "pirated" works undermine authors' interests in creating works by decreasing the value of the work or depriving the author of royalties, that free flow of creativity is stifled. Courts will measure the degree of such losses in their consideration of "fair use."

When a court decides whether to grant a "fair use" exemption, it will review all four factors. Additionally, the elements are not as broad as usually perceived. Religious organizations should never consider the "fair use" exemption as blanket permission to duplicate copyrighted material. In fact, they should consider "fair use" as a narrow, conservative exception.

Can the music director legally photocopy church hymns for performance at a meeting or worship service?

No, hymns may not be duplicated for wider distribution. The church's use would have to come clearly within one of the very narrow exemptions. The first exemption is fair use. The remaining two exemptions address *performances*.[7] These two exemptions are considered where hymns are *performed*, not copied or duplicated. Performances of a religious nature during the course of worship services or meetings may be exempt from copyright law, but *copies* made in order to prepare for performances may not. Hymns performed must meet the following criteria to qualify for exemption: they must be sung in the course of *worship* services or meetings, and the hymns must be religious in nature. Thus, performances for fund-raisers such as a "bingo night" would not meet the exemption requirements. The second performance exemption applies to nonprofit organizations. The *performance* of hymns meets the "nonprofit" requirement if there is no profit motive, no fee is paid to performers, and, if any admission fee is charged, the admission will fund only educational, religious, or charitable purposes.

Aside from the above-mentioned exemptions, copyrighted music or lyrics cannot be photocopied or reproduced in any way. This includes congregational use in a worship service. The written permission of the copyright owner is required. Additionally, it would be illegal to print songs in the church bulletins, make a song sheet, a songbook, overhead transparencies or slides, or record the worship service for a taped ministry. Written copyright permission would be essential.

There is a commercial way to solve this problem. For instance, Christian Copyright Licensing International (CCLI) offers a program in which a church can purchase a blanket license that allows the church access to most worship songs.[8] CCLI works with six hundred publishers who grant the right to use their music for noncommercial use. The copyright laws are designed to protect songwriters, and such a program assists in funneling the rightful royalties to the Christian songwriters.

What are the penalties for infringement?

Infringement includes use without permission, fraudulent copyright notice, fraudulent removal of a copyright notice, and a false representation on a copyright registration. The penalties are steep and statutorily set. Generally, civil damages consist of impounding the offending works, preventing further copying and distribution, and monetary damages for lost profits or royalties as well as court costs and attorney's fees.

If successful in court, the creator may elect either to receive *compensatory* damages or *statutory* damages. Compensatory damages are calculated by the losses or projected monetary losses due to the infringements. Statutory damages for a single infringement can be assessed from five hundred to twenty thousand dollars as the judge determines.

Willful violations are statutorily set at up to $100,000. "Willful" does not mean "malicious"; it means that the infringers knew or should have known that the copying was an infringement.[9]

Can a pastor use a quotation, passage, or verse from a copyrighted work in a sermon or talk without giving a reference?

This question goes to *plagiarism* as well as copyright infringement considerations. Plagiarists pretend that others' ideas are their own. Plagiarism does not necessarily involve the use of another's *copyrighted* material, but it can. Therefore, the Copyright Acts sanctions would not necessarily be applied against plagiarists. That is not to say, however, that there are no sanctions against plagiarism.

Such sanctions might include penalties from professional organizations as an ethical violation. It is rather easy to give verbal credit for the ideas of others when used in a sermon, for example. Thus it is easy to discharge this ethical duty.

Are there reference publications that might provide further information on this topic for clergy and religious organizations?

The following resources may be helpful in determining what materials a church may use without violating the Copyright Act:

Rightful Use by and available from

> Media Services of the United Presbyterian Church (USA)
> 100 Witherspoon St
> Louisville KY 40202
> 502.569.5212

This brief booklet covers the main copyright issues for churches including use of videos and video broadcasts.

Circular R1, "Copyright Basics," from the U.S. Copyright Office. This free booklet discusses the Copyright Office, registration of materials, copyright searches, and how to obtain further copyright documents and information.

Registrar of Copyrights
Library of Congress
Room 401
101 Independence Ave SE
Washington DC 20559
202.707.3000
202.707.9100 (forms hotline)

The Church Guide to Copyright Law by Richard R. Hammar, published by

Christian Ministry Resources
PO Box 2301
Matthews NC 28106
This larger work describes a full range of church copyright issues. Hammar describes cases and how they apply to copyright protection.

CHAPTER 6

Personal Injury

Actus dei nemini facir injuriam.
The law holds no man responsible for the act of God.
—R. H. Kersley
Broom's Legal Maxims

THE LAW MAY NOT HOLD a person liable for an act of God, but it certainly can hold one liable for poor judgment and ineptitude. Lawsuits alleging that someone has been personally injured through the fault of another are among the most common of all lawsuits. These so-called "slip-and-fall" cases are based on someone else's negligence. They often involve accidents to the victim such as slipping, falling, or twisted ankles that result from unsafe activities or unsafe premises. Negligence actions (also called "torts") are based on the allegation that the defendant is legally responsible for causing the injury because he or she did something that he or she should not have done or failed to do something that he or she should have done. The basic legal elements of a personal injury case are as follows:[1]

A legal duty is the first element. A legal (not moral) duty either to do something or refrain from doing something must be established to prevail in a tort suit. In U.S. law most people have a duty to conduct themselves and others and objects for which they are responsible in such a way as not to injure another. One must drive his or her car or walk his or her dog such that no harm comes to innocent bystanders.

A breach of that duty is the second element. The injured party must prove that the person in question abrogated his or her duty to the injured person in some way.

Damages are the third element. Some tangible harm must be shown. Today many courts include both physical and mental or emotional injury as potential harm. Of course property damage fulfills the damage requirement.

A causal connection ("proximate cause") linking the damages to the breach of duty is the fourth element. A person who is injured must prove that the alleged breach of duty resulted in the damages he or she has sustained.

Each of the four elements must be proven for a plaintiff (injured party) to prevail in a negligence case.

Can a parishioner sue the religious institution and prevail if he or she slips on spilt milk in the fellowship hall?

Assuming that "charitable immunity," discussed in chapter 1, does not apply in this case, the plaintiff could sue the religious institution. A Pennsylvania court found that a parishioner failed to prove the four elements mentioned above and dismissed a suit against her priest, church, and diocese. She had slipped on snow and ice as she walked through the church parking lot to attend a bingo game held at the church.[2] The court ruled that the woman had to show that there were accumulations of snow and ice in ridges and elevations that obstructed her ability to walk in the parking lot, thereby constituting a danger to her. The court also ruled that she had to prove that the parish had active or constructive notice of the dangerous ridges and elevations of snow and ice and failed to act.

The parishioner who falls on spilt milk in the fellowship hall must also prove the four elements. First, the parishioner must prove that the religious organization has a duty to protect him or her from slipping. For instance, was the parishioner supposed to be there at that time? The parishioner would have to prove that the religious organization had breached a duty to maintain safe premises. Specifically the religious institution would have to: (1) know that someone had spilt milk; (2) know that the milk posed a danger because people in the fellowship hall were likely to slip; and (3) act in a timely fashion to clean up such spills.

Damages are the next element. The plaintiff would have to prove that he or she suffered damages. A broken bone and medical bills would certainly prove that an injury existed. Finally, the plaintiff would need to establish that the injury was caused by a fall in the church and not while playing golf.

Many states hold a property owner to different degrees of duty depending on the status of the person who enters the property. The duty owed to an uninvited entrant is less than the duty owed to someone invited to the fellowship hall by the religious group. In other words, a burglar breaking into the fellowship hall to steal the microwave is not entitled to the same standard of care that is extended to an invited guest. The religious group owes a higher standard of care to the electrician who is asked to enter the fellowship hall to repair the microwave. Thus if a burglar slips on spilt milk while burglarizing the fellowship hall and is injured, he or she may have little legal recourse unless the church placed patently dangerous obstacles in his or her path.

The courts will look at many factors to determine the liability of the church such as: (1) the purpose for which the entrant came onto the premises; (2) the circumstances under which the entrant came onto the premises; (3) the expected use of the premises; (4) the foreseeability or possibility of harm; (5) the reasonableness of inspection or warning; and (6) the opportunity and ease of repair.[3]

A court in Minnesota held that a motorcyclist, mistakenly entering church property, was entitled to a higher standard of care than a "trespasser."[4] The church was located at a juncture of two roads. The church entrance was often mistaken by motorists for a through highway. There had been prior accidents near the church, and the church had erected signs warning of the dangerous entrance, which were subsequently removed. The church erected a dirt berm to discourage through traffic onto its property. A motorcyclist was injured when he hit the dirt berm. The court held that the church was liable because the church knew or should have known of the dangerous condition. The church's duty included warning vehicular traffic of the dangerous dirt berm on the church's property.

Given these factors, religious institutions may owe a high standard of care to nonmembers who use the premises for nonreligious reasons such as Alcoholics Anonymous meetings and other self-help groups, community meetings, neighbors who walk their dogs on church property, neighbors who use the playground, or kids who use the parking lot or the handicap ramp for skateboarding.

Can a religious organization be successfully sued if the person driving the youth group back to the church from the roller rink gets into a car accident?

Generally, a parent may prevail against a religious organization if the driver of the youth group car was found to be negligent. A successful negligence suit can be maintained if the four necessary elements for negligence, discussed above, are satisfied. There is, however, an additional concern. The driver and owner of the vehicle and his or her relationship to the religious organization are crucial considerations in assessing legal liability under these circumstances. If the vehicle is owned and operated by the religious organization, then there is little question that the religious group is liable—assuming that the driver is found negligent.

The necessary elements of *respondeat superior*, discussed in chapters 8 and 10, would need to be invoked in order to hold the religious body legally responsible for the negligent acts of a driver who was a parent driving his or her own car, for instance. *Respondeat superior* considers such questions as: did the driver use the vehicle at the request of or for the benefit of the religious organization, and did the driver act within the parameters of instruction or guidance or within the "scope" of his or her employment. If the court or jury rules that the state requirements have been met, the religious organization could be held liable.

Are there some general types of behavior over which churches are repeatedly sued?

There are three types of torts for which churches are repeatedly sued: (1) car, van, and bus accidents; (2) sexual molestation of youth; and (3) ladder and scaffolding accidents. The first two often involve the improper conduct of unpaid volunteers. The third category involves the church's poor judgment regarding dangerous activities. Even if the church were bereft of a healthy respect for legal liability, the church has a moral interest in protecting the health and welfare of its members. Yet the number of cases where a parishioner is injured in an accident related to ladders or scaffolding is startling.

These cases generally involve a pastor's attempt to save money and his or her request for volunteers from the congregation to undertake some job for the church such as trimming trees, fixing a roof, adhering ceiling tiles, or installing fans. A volunteer is subsequently seriously injured falling from a ladder or scaffolding and sues the church. The court will determine whether the church had asked for volunteers and had requested that they do the specific job in question. The court will review whether the church suggested the methods and provided the materials.

In one case, the church was aware that a ladder was being set up on the pews.[5] The wife of the injured party sued both the pastor and the church, alleging that they subjected her husband to an open and obvious danger; failed to provide a safe, suitable, and proper ladder for his support and weight; and failed to use reasonable care in overseeing his work. She also invoked two state statutes. The wife claimed that the defendants had violated the structural work act, which protected anyone engaged on a ladder while undertaking the repair of a building. She also claimed that they violated the Illinois premises liability act, which required land possessors to use reasonable care to protect entrants. Thus in addition to general tort law, churches and religious leaders may be found liable for such incidents under state statutes specifically designed to prevent and protect workers from these types of accidents.

Even in cases where the negligence was caused by another volunteer, the court may find that proper supervision by the church may well have averted the accident. Often the volunteers are unfamiliar with the equipment. The church normally will be in a position to purchase or provide safety equipment and promote safety. Hiring at least one professional for supervisory purposes would be advisable. Moreover, it stands to reason that the church should not encourage folly. In one case the church provided a few bottles of "altar wine" for refreshment while the volunteers were undertaking dangerous activities.[6]

Would it be legal to tape-record a private counseling session and not to tell the counselee?

Every state has its own laws regarding surreptitious tape recording. In California, for example, the state privacy act prohibits one party to a conversation from recording it without the other's consent. This is particularly true when the communications are confidential. [7]

Federal statute prohibits surreptitious recording without a person's knowledge or consent.[8] It requires, however, proof that the "recorder" made the recording with the intent to commit a criminal or otherwise injurious act. If such an element can be proven, damages can be quite substantial. One man received a jury award of $183,000.[9] The court found that the man who made the recording not only violated the federal statute but also violated a common law right against invasion of privacy in which the victim had a reasonable expectation of privacy about his conversation.

The state of Washington flatly prohibits the recording of a private conversation without first obtaining the consent of the persons involved in the conversation. The minister should make it clear to all the parties engaged in the conversation that the communication is about to be recorded. This announcement should be recorded as a part of the tape.[10]

Needless to say, even with the counselee's permission, making tape recordings requires a high degree of caution. These tapes must be kept under lock and key. If these communications were to be publicly disclosed, even by a third party, the counselor would be vulnerable to suit.

What is clergy "malpractice"?

Clergy malpractice is a specific term for professional negligence applicable to clergypersons. Almost everyone has heard of medical malpractice or legal malpractice. Clergy malpractice means that a clergyperson has performed his or her duties below an established standard of care. This standard is established by examining the prevailing practice of similar religious professionals. To date, no court has allowed a claim specifically for clergy malpractice.

Recently a federal district court in New York State carefully discussed clergy malpractice.[11] The court considered whether sexual relations between a Presbyterian minister and a counseling client constituted "clergy malpractice." The court ruled that it would recognize no such claim against the minister.

First, the court found that counseling was a normal part of clerical duties. Second, as a normal part of religious duties, this religious function was fundamentally different from the counseling of other human services professionals. This fundamental difference was established by the fact that there was no verifiable standard of care for "reasonable clergy" conducting counseling. To affix a standard of care for a Presbyterian minister would cause the court to entangle itself in the affairs of a religious group. Indeed the court would become the ruling authority over the church on proper clergy behavior. Such a decision would result in excessive entanglement between the church and state and would be constitutionally impermissible.

This is not to say, however, that courts will not hold clergy legally accountable for sexual misconduct or other alleged wrongdoing under a number of other legal theories. Courts have found clergy liable under similar facts for fraud, breach of fiduciary duty, breach of contract, and other legal bases of liability.

How much clergy malpractice insurance should a clergyperson or religious organization maintain?

As a rule, *both* clergy and religious organizations should have insurance covering negligent acts and maybe even misconduct. The coverage should account for regional differences in the costs of obtaining an attorney and the costs of losing such suits, as well as the amount and type of counseling and other interpersonal work conducted by clergy. Coverage of at least one million dollars is not uncommon. The policy should include coverage for legal fees. Religious organizations may want to obtain coverage for their directors and officers as well.

The clergyperson should carry *personal* liability insurance. Personal coverage is available from such groups as the American Counseling Association, the National Association of Social Workers, and other professional organizations. Carrying personal insurance in addition to that obtained by the religious organization is important because the organization's policy probably covers only the organization itself. Moreover, sometimes the interests of the religious organization and the clergy are identical; sometimes they are not. For example, the church may want to "settle" a suit (make an out-of-court financial arrangement with the complaining party). This settlement may be good for the organization in reduced costs and reduced publicity, but it may leave lingering doubts about the fault or guilt of the clergyperson.

If an insurance company refuses to pay a claim in bad faith, punitive damages may be awarded to the policyholder by the court. Religious institutions and religious professionals should be familiar with the contents of their insurance policies. An insurer's duty to defend the policyholder is determined by comparing the policy coverage provisions with the allegations brought against the policyholder. The insurer's duty to defend is broader than its duty to indemnify. In situations in which the pastor admits culpability, the insurance carrier may still be obligated to defend the church, religious leader, association, conference, or denomination. Additionally, many policies require timely notification if a suit is filed against the church or religious professional; otherwise the coverage may be denied.

The church should maintain hazard insurance, personal injury insurance, building insurance, and clergy malpractice insurance. The extent of coverage will depend on the size of the church, the amount of land, and the scope of building and land usage.

Will "agreements not to sue" signed by parents or guardians protect religious organizations from being sued?

"Agreements not to sue" are universally disavowed by U.S. courts. Nonetheless, many religious institutions routinely ask the parents of young people and children to sign permission slips when they go on field trips, youth retreats, and so on. Many of these documents also include language designed to release the religious institution, drivers, or chaperones from liability should an accident occur. These releases and permission slips are essentially contracts in which parents or guardians purport to bargain away their right to sue in exchange for the privilege of attending the function. Such contracts to release another from liability in personal injury actions are universally prohibited as against public policy.[12] No one is allowed to preempt another's right to sue for personal injury.

Religious organizations are better served by requiring all participants to sign *indemnification* agreements. Indemnification agreements are contracts whereby a participant in a church activity agrees to repay or to indemnify the organization for any money it may lose through suits brought by the participant against the church for personal injury. Those parents whose children win a personal injury suit against a religious organization will reimburse the organization for monies the organization paid as a result of the litigation. Such contracts preserve the right to sue of the person harmed while allowing the organization to reclaim any damage award it had to pay. The religious leader should consult an attorney for the validity of indemnification agreements in his or her respective state.

The language of an indemnification contract might begin this way:

In consideration of being accepted by [religious organization] for participation in [activity], we (I), being 21 years or older, on behalf of [minor child] do hereby agree to hold harmless from, indemnify, and defend against, including the payment of attorney's fees, the [religious organization], its trustees, ministers, officers, and volunteers, including volunteers pertaining to the above trip or activity, any and all claims, liability, allegations of personal injury, sickness, or death, as well as property damages and expenses, of any nature whatsoever that may be incurred by the undersigned and/or child participant that may occur while said child is participating in the above-described trip or activity.

Furthermore, we (I) (and on behalf or our [my] child participant [if under the age of 21 years]) hereby assume all risk of personal injury, sickness, death, damage, and expense as a result of participation in the recreation and work activities involved herein.

This document should, of course, be used in conjunction with authorization to attend the function, authorization for emergency medical treatment, and other authorizations.

CHAPTER 7

Defamation

Ubi jus ibi remedium.
There is no wrong without a remedy.

—R. H. Kersley
Broom's Legal Maxims

THE LAW PROVIDES that it will guard against defamation, an insult to a person's reputation. The court shall extend a remedy of compensation to the victim and a remedy of punishment to the defamer should such a wrong be proven in court. Thus clergy need to be very sensitive about such legal wrongs as in the following hypothetical situation.

A clergy has a counseling session with a couple seeking to be married. After the initial counseling session, the clergy refuses to marry them, saying that they are too immature and insensitive to each other. The clergy tells the secretary to cancel the remaining counseling appointments with them, explaining that "they are just too selfish."

To *defame* someone means to harm his or her reputation by perpetrating a falsehood that harms his or her standing in the community. Defamation includes two classes of legal liability: slander and libel. Generally slander involves harm to another's reputation by use of the spoken word, and libel involves harm to another's reputation by use of the printed word. Traditionally courts considered *libel* to be the more serious offense because the printed word could theoretically reach a wider audience. With today's technology of radio, video, and cable access, the legal distinctions between libel and slander have become blurred if not abolished.

Clergy are vulnerable to being sued for defaming others. Most clergy speak with tens, even hundreds, of people every week. Congregational members or others discuss sensitive issues often concerning the characters and actions of others. Clergy form opinions of others and their behavior. If these opinions are communicated to others, they may form allegations of defamation. The cases that follow illustrate some of these concerns.

State statutes control defamation, but the requirements for defamation are similar throughout the states. The basic requirements to win a defamation case are: (1) the existence of a defamatory statement, (2) it has been published, (3) it is false, (4) the defamer has acted with actual or implied malice (reckless disregard for the truth or with ill will), and (5) there is resultant injury.[1] Defamation per se takes place when a statement is so damaging that no proof of damages is required. An example of this would be calling a local minister an adulterer and a thief. Defamation *pro quid* requires proof of damages.

All five elements are necessary for a plaintiff to succeed in a suit for defamation. For example, defamatory *thoughts* do not rise to the level of defamation because no one hears them. The second element of publication is necessary because others need to learn of the defamatory statements or writings. Of course the statements must be proven to be false. Usually the damaging publications need to be made maliciously or with reckless disregard for the truth. Finally, if no harm (lowering of reputation) occurs, the suit will not succeed.

Should a religious organization or a religious leader publish in its newsletter the reasons for firing the church secretary?

To avoid suit by a disgruntled former employee, good legal advice would be to *never* publish the reason for any church-related employment decision, particularly firing decisions. If the religious organization decides that it wants to make public the basis for the firing, however, the basis must be accurate, verifiable, and not made with any evil intent. Consent to such publication from the employee would of course be ideal.

An Ohio appeals court held that publicly disclosing reasons for termination may state a valid claim for defamation.[2] Catherine Davis was a church secretary for ten years before Father Fisher arrived as church rector. After six months she asserted sexual harassment complaints against Fisher to the church and the diocese. Davis' claims were unresolved by the church or the diocese. Finally, the chancellor of the diocese advised Fisher to fire Davis. The church did so and then asked Fisher to place an article in the church newsletter to explain the firing. Fisher wrote an article stating that Davis was fired for engaging in openly malicious behavior to discredit him.

Davis sued the church, the diocese, and Fisher asserting several theories, including intentional and negligent infliction of emotional distress, retaliatory discharge, and defamation. The appeals court found that her suit stated some of the necessary elements for pleading defamation, that is, publication (in the church newsletter) and the statements, if proven untrue, could be injurious. The existence of malice, decided the court, was a factual question that the trial court had to consider.

The court then turned to the issue of whether a mere opinion could rise to the level of defamation. The general rule is that opinions are *not* actionable *unless* they are made with a reckless disregard for the truth or are made with knowledge of their falsity. In this case the court ruled that the "opinion defense" must be decided as a factual matter. Thus the trial court had to hear evidence about whether Fisher published his opinion of the firing in order to maliciously discredit Davis.

The court then considered *who* would be legally accountable for writing the allegedly defamatory remarks in the newsletter. Davis sued the diocese (as well as the church and Fisher) for defamation, claiming that the diocese told Fisher what to write in the allegedly defamatory newsletter. Under this theory Davis was hoping to hold both Fisher and the diocese responsible. The court concluded, however, that the church's newsletter was controlled by the church and by Fisher—and only by them—saying, "The fact that the chancellor gave extremely poor legal advice does not give rise to the claim of . . . defamation."[3]

Can the worship leader be sued if he or she, in a sermon, inadvertently calls someone a habitual liar or other such term?

A worship leader who calls someone a liar or other such term is likely to be sued for defamation. Such a statement may meet the five requirements of defamation. First, being called a liar usually damages the reputation. Second, the statement would be "published"—with a congregation full of witnesses. Third, as a defense, it would be up to the clergy to prove that the statement was true. Fourth, it would be up to the victim to prove malice, which means ill will or reckless disregard for the truth if the remark were inadvertent. Fifth, damages could probably be proven even if the harm arising from the defamation was not readily apparent. Two cases can help illustrate the types of statements that might be considered defamatory.

In one unusual case the court found that the pastor intended to harm a family with his defamatory remarks. In *Hester v. Barnett*, an appeals court in Missouri ruled that statements made in sermons, church bulletins, conversation, and letters set forth a justifiable claim of defamation.[4] The alleged defamatory statements included charges that a husband and wife beat, whipped, and abused their children and used them to get work done. The pastor stated that the husband cheated the government and was an arsonist, a thief, and did not pay his employees their earned wages.

Another case involved letters written by one minister about another minister's conduct as a missionary in Japan.[5] The minister accused the missionary of stealing, failing to pay debts, and carrying out "Satan's plan" of dividing churches. The court ruled that such statements were libelous. When a clergyman or clergywoman's honesty, trustworthiness, or morality is impugned, his or her reputation is almost certainly damaged.

There have been several instances in which a person's alleged immorality has been discussed with the congregation from the pulpit as part of the church's beliefs regarding repentance and shunning. When this type of information is gleaned from a confession, the church should be very careful not to invade the person's privacy or to abuse a confidence that the congregant has placed in the person hearing the confession.

In one case a bishop confessed to his assistant archbishop of the Holy Synod of the Evangelical Orthodox Church that he was having an affair with a member of the congregation.[6] The bishop was promised that his confession would be kept in strict confidence. The congregant made a similar confession to the diocesan bishop and was also promised confidentiality. The love affair, however, was announced on Sunday by the church to the congregation. Those who were not present were informed in person at their homes. The bishop and the congregant sued the church and the specific individuals for invasion of privacy, breach of fiduciary duty, emotional distress, malpractice, and interference with prospective economic advantage, injurious falsehood, conspiracy, and so forth.

The church stated that its behavior was not reviewable by the court because it involved religious practices and beliefs that the court had no power to regulate. The court disagreed because it determined that the interests invaded by the church might be sufficiently significant to warrant state protection. Therefore, while truth may be a complete defense to a suit for defamation, the victim may sue alleging other types of harm instead of damage to the reputation. The court may find that the alleged harm is important enough to require state protection.

If a minister is fired because he or she "is unable to conduct his or her ministry efficiently," can such a statement be a basis for a defamation action?

In *Black v. Snyder*, a federal trial court ruled that it could not review the falsity of a statement involving a minister's efficiency.[7] An associate pastor was fired after bringing sexual harassment charges against the senior pastor. The church stated the reason for her discharge as "inability to conduct her ministry efficiently."

The associate pastor sued, claiming that the remarks defamed her. The court reasoned that this claim would necessarily involve a review of why she was discharged. The court then decided that such a review would involve the court in an essentially ecclesiastical matter—impermissible under the First Amendment provisions separating church and state.

Although a church may have legitimate concerns about an employee's immorality, will discussion of this subject the church to suits for defamation?

The court will review the facts of each case to determine if ecclesiastical concerns form the heart of the alleged defamation. Where a body of rabbis published a notice stating that a plaintiff was a bigamist according to Jewish religious standards and advised shunning, the court refused to inquire into religious doctrine and practice.[8] If the matter is viewed as the province of civil law, the court will decide issues of defamation.

Pastor Buchenroth came across files of the church's other pastor, Reverend Shaheen, which contained personal correspondence with a female youth worker, Ms. Smith.[9] Buchenroth thought the letters were proof of a sexual relationship between Shaheen and Smith. Buchenroth showed the letters to several people, including church staff members, Shaheen's father, and Smith's mother. Smith began to receive unsettling phone calls, was dismissed from her church job, was subjected to scorn in her church, and was unable to find another job commensurate with her skills. Although Buchenroth thereafter seemed convinced his allegations were false and apologized to both Shaheen and Smith, he repeated his earlier allegations to some church members.

Smith sued Buchenroth and the church for defamation and invasion of privacy and won a judgment of both compensatory and punitive damages. Compensatory damages reimburse the victim for expenses that have been caused by the defamatory statements. In this case Smith was fired from her job and precluded from finding another suitable position. The judge awarded her a compensatory judgment of $228,904.

Punitive damages were awarded to deter future defamatory acts on the part of the defendant pastor and church. Punitive damages can be limited by state law. These awards are determined by the judge or the jury and can often exceed compensatory judgments. The court awarded Smith punitive damages of $2,000 against Buchenroth and $105,875 against the church.

How can a religious organization protect itself from being defamed?

A religious organization can protect its reputation by bringing suit *immediately* once it finds that it has been defamed. The church should not wait until the information is widely disseminated but should enforce its rights at the very first publication of the libelous information. Otherwise it may lose its right of legal redress because of the statute of limitations.

In a 1978 case the Church of Scientology of Minnesota claimed that an article published in *Today's Health*, a publication of the American Medical Association, contained defamatory statements.[10] The title of the article was, "Scientology—Menace to Mental Health."

A newspaper in St. Paul, Minnesota, received a reprint of the original article and published it as a column. The court ruled that the "single publication rule" would govern the case. The date of the *original* publication would start the two-year statute of limitations, and no future republication would extend the time limit within which to file a defamation suit. Some courts have ruled that *each* publication or republication will recommence the running of the statute of limitations. In Minnesota, when the first defamatory statement is published, the suit must be filed within two years.

The court found that the article was indeed defamatory on its face because "charging another with fraud and dishonesty are defamatory regardless of the terms in which they are couched."[11] The court, however, ruled against the church on the ground that the defamatory claim was not brought within the two-year statute of limitations.

If a religious leader brings a suit for defamation, should he or she also bring a suit for infliction of emotional distress?

Yes. The elements are similar such that if the religious leader can prove defamation, he or she can probably prove intentional infliction of emotional distress. Probably the most famous case of defamation involving a religious figure is *Hustler Magazine, Inc., v. Falwell*.[12] Rev. Jerry Falwell sued *Hustler* magazine and its publisher Larry Flynt for defamation, invasion of privacy, and intentional infliction of emotional distress. The case centered around *Hustler*'s parody of a national ad wherein celebrities described their "first time" drinking Campari Liqueur. Copying the overall format of the Campari ads, Hustler printed a fictitious interview with Falwell detailing his "first time"— but with a twist. The fictitious interview implied that Falwell was describing a drunken, incestuous incident in an outhouse with his mother. At the bottom of the page, a disclaimer read: "ad parody—not to be taken seriously."

Falwell *did* take the ad seriously and sued in federal court. *Hustler* and Flynt won both the invasion of privacy and defamation claims. The jury found that the parody could not reasonably be taken seriously. In other words, a reasonable person would recognize that the ad did not portray the truth. Falwell, however, won $100,000 in compensatory damages and $50,000 from each of the defendants on the emotional distress claim. The federal court of appeals affirmed the judgment.

The Supreme Court issued an opinion that surprised everyone. It held, in contravention of the two lower courts, that the right to free speech prohibits "public figures" from winning suits for intentional infliction of emotional distress without proving "actual" malice. This means that Falwell had to prove that *Hustler* or Flynt knew the parody was false but portrayed the parody as true or with "reckless disregard" for the truth such that a reasonable person would be misled. Indeed as the following appeals court testimony shows,[13] Flynt had ill will toward Falwell. However, even when the defamer intends to harm the victim, where the public recognizes the published statement is false, no claim will succeed. The questioning below is from case testimony:

Q: Did you want to upset Reverend Falwell?

Flynt: Yes.

Q: Do you recognize that, in having published what you did in this ad, you were attempting to convey to the people who read it that Reverend Falwell was just as you characterized him, a liar?

Flynt: He's a glutton.

Q: How about a liar?

Flynt: Yeah, he's a liar, too.

Q: How about a hypocrite?

Flynt: Yeah.

Q: That's what you wanted to convey?

Flynt: Yeah.

Q: And didn't it occur to you that if it wasn't true, you were attacking a man in his profession?

Flynt: Yes.

Q: Did you appreciate, at the time you wrote "okay" or approved this publication, that for Reverend Falwell to function in his livelihood and in his commitment and career, he has to have an integrity that people believe in? Did you appreciate that?

Flynt: Yeah.

Thus even though Flynt wanted to publicly humiliate Falwell, his intention did not rise to the level of "actual malice" because the public recognized that the cartoon was a parody. The court created this higher "actual malice" standard in intentional infliction of emotional distress cases where a person's constitutional right to free speech is at risk regarding a public figure. The Supreme Court noted Falwell's "public figure" status by saying, "[Falwell] is the host of a nationally syndicated television show and is the founder and president of a political organization formerly known as the Moral Majority. He is also the founder of Liberty University . . . and the author of several books and publications."[14]

Most religious leaders neither seek nor reach such public visibility. To be parodied on the national level, the religious professional needs repeated national visibility. Local publicity through newspaper articles or otherwise will not result in "public figure" status. A local religious figure could probably have prevailed in Falwell's suit because he or she would not have had to prove actual malice as an element of the intentional infliction of emotional distress claim.

What defenses can a religious institution or religious leader raise if they are sued for defamation?

In defamation suits, as in other legal cases, affirmative defenses are available to the defendant.

Employers

Absolute or qualified immunities or privileges may be defenses. For instance, employers may have a limited immunity when giving pertinent employee information to prospective employers. Courts recognize that prospective employers have a legitimate interest in receiving frank and honest employee recommendations. Thus employers who offer another employer an honest, unmalicious, and verifiable recommendation will qualify for a limited privilege to give their opinion on the employee's job performance.

A former employer reported to a consumer agency (prospective boss) that its former employee was "wholly incompetent" and "ineligible for rehire." The employee sued for defamation. The court found that the employee had lied about his qualifications on his job application, had conflicts with other employees resulting in at least one fist fight, and had walked off his job without giving notice. The court ruled in favor of the former employer for three reasons: (1) the opinions in the former employer's report were not false; (2) they were made without malice; and (3) they were covered by the employer's qualified privilege.[15]

Communications in the course of official church business enjoy this *qualified* privilege.[16] Duly constituted committees considering candidates have a limited right to open and frank discussion of the candidate's qualifications. This privilege has limitations. These communications must be confined to the candidate's behavior directly connected to holding religious office. Someone sharing information strictly about a candidate's personal life would not be granted the immunity. Furthermore, the statements must be made without malice—that is, the person sharing the information must have reasonable grounds to believe that the statements are true. At this point it might be helpful to point out how quickly a discussion of a person's character or qualifications can move beyond verifiable facts and become tainted by overbroad descriptions or colorful adjectives.

Good Faith Child Abuse Reporting

A "good faith" immunity applies to suspected child abuse reporting where the person thought he or she was telling the truth—*even though* he or she was wrong.[17] The Supreme Court of South Dakota determined that the good faith privilege applied to a false report of child abuse.[18] Parents who suspected their daughter's boyfriend's parents of abusing him reported their suspicions to the Department of Social Services. The boyfriend's parents sued for defamation. The court determined that the girl's parents demonstrated concern for the boyfriend and that the report was motivated out of such concern.

Many religious-school teachers ask if they are required to report suspected incidences of child abuse. Sunday-school teachers are one of society's first line of professionals who have regular contact with children and possible knowledge of abuse. All states will *allow* such teachers to report suspected abuse and will immunize the teacher for any erroneous report made in good faith. To make a report the teacher does not have to have absolute proof. Some states *require* public and private school-teachers to report cases of suspected child abuse. The church worker will want to check the state statute closely to determine whether he or she is required to report suspected child abuse. If they are required, then they will be in violation of the law if they fail to report their suspicions. These teachers must review the statute to determine whom they must report to and whether they must do so within a very short time frame.

The Constitution

The *Black v. Snyder* court mentioned above ruled that the free exercise clause discussed in chapter 3 prohibited it from interfering with church employment decisions to fire a minister even if the reasons for those decisions were published. The court, however, also ruled that the free exercise clause did not preclude the minister from claiming either sexual harassment or wrongful termination under the state "whistleblower" laws.

What are some rules of thumb to assist religious leaders and institutions in avoiding charges of defamation?

The easiest way to avoid defamation suits is to avoid disclosing information that is either insupportable by verifiable data or is confidential. It goes without saying that a parishioner or employee should not be discussed in a spirit of anger, vindictiveness, or gossip.

Religious organizations are involved in several kinds of confidential communications. Clergy and other religious professionals are persons to whom people turn in times of crisis and personal turmoil. In counseling situations both the process and the content of the client's (or parishioner's) discussions should be kept private. Storytelling about clients, including pastoral diagnosis or assessment and other "interesting" anecdotes about those who seek the help of religious professionals, are fertile ground for defamation and other legal suits. Gossip, even "professional" gossip, begs for litigation. Any disclosure of clients' circumstances should take place with their written consent. Even when a parishioner is not a counselee per se, the religious leader learns many intimate details of a parishioner's life, which must not be disclosed. A passion for discretion is the best tonic for defamation.

Another fertile area for defamation claims involves evaluations of past and current employees or volunteers. Conducting informal employee evaluations among coworkers or others only attracts mistrust and defamation claims. Discussion of an employee's performance should be conducted with great discretion. Employee evaluations should only include those parties organizationally directed to be involved. The written results of such evaluations should be limited to authorized persons with instructions that the information be kept confidential.

CHAPTER 8

Employment and Labor Law

Respondeat superior.
Let the principal be held responsible.

—R. H. Kersley
Broom's Legal Maxims

THE DOCTRINE OF *respondeat superior* holds the employer legally responsible in monetary damages for the wrongful acts of his or her employees or agents acting within the scope of their employment duties. Employer liability is predicated on the reasoning that the risk of damage or injury is best borne by the one who is benefiting from the employment relationship and the one in the best position to prevent the wrongful acts. One court upheld a punitive-damage award of $2.7 million against a diocese and archdiocese of St. Paul and Minneapolis because they showed a willful indifference or deliberate lack of concern for others by trying to hide that one of their priests had a twenty-three-year history of molesting boys.[1]

Employment and labor law is an area of expanding liability that has direct relevance for spiritual leaders. Churches must comply with federal and state employment and labor laws, including the Fair Labor Standards Act, the Civil Rights Acts, and laws against sexual harassment.

What is vicarious employer liability (*respondeat superior*), and how can religious organizations protect themselves from such liability?

Vicarious employer liability involves various legal bases for making the employer or supervisor legally responsible for the acts of employees. Employers owe a duty to the public to properly hire and supervise employees in such a way that the employees do the public no harm.

Imposing expanding liability on the employer hinges on how the court defines an employee's "scope of employment." If the offending act is determined to be within an employee's scope of employment, the employer will be liable for the employee's conduct. If the act is determined to be outside the scope of employment, the employer will not be held responsible for the employee's conduct. Consistent with vicarious employer liability, a court in *Byrd v. Faber* held that a church and governing body could not be held liable for the wrongful acts of its employee if those acts were not committed within the scope of employment.[2] The court then took a narrow view of the *scope of employment* concept.

Mr. and Mrs. Byrd attended a church to which Reverend Faber had been assigned by the leadership of the Seventh Day Adventists. During the course of their attendance, the Byrds asked Faber to counsel them regarding their marriage and personal problems. The Byrds alleged that during the course of such counseling, Faber coerced Mrs. Byrd into having sexual relations with him. The Byrds sued the minister for malpractice, fraud, intentional infliction of emotional distress, and nonconsensual sexual conduct.

The couple also sued the pastor's state and national church organizations, alleging that they were liable pursuant to the *respondeat superior* doctrine. The Supreme Court of Ohio found that sexual misconduct is *intentional* conduct as opposed to a mere act of negligence. An intentional tort is a harmful act conducted with deliberation and foresight; a negligent act might include forgetting to scrape ice off steps or neglecting to repair broken handrails. The court trying the Byrd case found that the employee's intentional acts would be within the scope of employee duties only if the acts "facilitate or promote" church business. Faber's employers did not hire him "to rape, seduce, or otherwise physically assault members of his congregation." As superiors in Faber's denomination did not promote or advocate his action, no liability could be assigned to them.

The minister's alleged conduct also must be foreseeable by his employers. To fulfill the "foreseeability" requirement, Faber's employers must have had some reason to predict Faber's alleged acts. The Byrds claimed that the Ohio Conference and others knew or should have known that Faber had an "inclination" to commit such acts. However, they offered no proof of such claims. Thus liability under *respondeat superior* was denied.

Not all courts have used this more narrow interpretation of *scope of employment*. The Supreme Court of Alaska held that a religious counselor's intercourse with a client one month after the client terminated therapy was within the religious counselor's scope of employment; thus the court held the religious counseling center liable for the acts of a minister-therapist.[3] Even though actual intercourse took place outside the counseling premises and after the counseling had ended, the employer counseling center was held responsible for the minister's action.

The court ruled that the counselor's conduct within therapy (fondling and kissing) could be characterized as initiating intercourse. Additionally the court held that it would be reasonable to conclude that the minister's mishandling of the transference phenomena *during* counseling facilitated the sexual misconduct. This ruling may be a harbinger for greater employer liability.

The religious organization must be very attentive when it hires an employee. It must call references and do a thorough check of the person's background. If the church knows or should know that a person has a history of criminal behavior, toward children for example, the church is under an obligation to use that information in such a way as to protect its congregants. Moreover, a church is under a duty to supervise its employees very carefully to ensure that they are conducting themselves in accordance with the religious organization's wishes.

There are additional factors apart from those discussed above that the courts will review in assessing the proper definition of the scope of employment of a religious employee (minister or other employee). First, courts will scrutinize the nature of the employee's relationship to the employer to determine the degree of independence enjoyed by the employee. The courts will closely examine the employment contract or agreement of the religious employee to determine the nature and extent to which the employee's duties are controlled by the church governing body.

Second, often a religious body has the power to suspend or withdraw clergy credentials, pay for rehabilitation, or help the clergy find employment; courts may consider such ties to be evidence of a continual relationship substantial enough to hold the religious group vicariously liable. Even though clergy often have wide discretion in their work and sometimes have minimal supervision by either their parishes or their religious organizations, both their immediate employers (church, synagogue, or other body) *and* their religious hierarchy or denomination can be held liable.

Must religious organizations abide by the Fair Labor Standards Act (FLSA), which requires payment of a minimum wage and pay equity?

Places of worship, as such, are not covered by the FLSA, which governs employee working hours and minimum-wage requirements. The FLSA does cover nonprofit schools and organizations engaged in business or commercial enterprises. The Supreme Court has held that some religious businesses are *commercial or business enterprises*, therefore these enterprises come within the jurisdiction of the FLSA.[4] Generally when religious beliefs or strictly theological positions are not at issue, the federal wage requirements must be met. *The Tony and Susan Alamo Foundation v. Secretary of Labor* case involved a foundation that, instead of paying employee wages, gave the employees (rehabilitated drug addicts, homeless people, and criminals) food, clothing, and shelter. The foundation claimed that religious convictions precluded the employees from accepting wages. The court ruled that the foundation was an enterprise because it competed with other secular businesses. The foundation derived its income from its operation of service stations, retail clothing stores, grocery outlets, farms, construction companies, motels, and candy companies. Therefore the foundation was required to abide by the FLSA standards.

Preschools and schools operated by religious organizations are covered by the FLSA.[5] A federal court of appeals held that a school violated the FLSA both by failing to pay teachers the minimum wage and by failing to pay female teachers comparable wages for the same work that male teachers were performing. The church-operated school could not seek exemption from the FLSA by designating its teachers as "ministers." It is worth noting that religious organizations must pay Social Security taxes for their employees. They should check their state law to determine if they are required to pay unemployment insurance and workers compensation.

Must religious organizations abide by the Civil Rights Act, which prohibits discrimination in hiring and employment practices?

The Civil Rights Act of 1964 and its amendments protect people from employment discrimination based on race, sex, creed, ethnic background, and age. Title VII of the 1964 Civil Rights Act exempts religious institutions from its constraints when they carry out their religious purposes. The Roman Catholic Church may choose to hire only *males* for its priesthood without fear of violating the antidiscrimination laws because of its *theological* position against ordaining female priests.

A religious organization may discriminate on the basis of religion or religious values in its employment practices. A Presbyterian presbytery or Methodist conference, for example, may refuse to ordain a person whose theological views conflict with those of the church.

Courts give religious bodies wide legal latitude regarding employment decisions on clergy. In one case a Methodist minister filed suit against his annual conference, claiming age discrimination when he was placed with a congregation that was not commensurate with his training and experience.[6] The court ruled that church appointments must take into account the unique needs of the charge and the gifts and graces of a particular pastor. Therefore the decision was based on religious factors and would not be subject to court review.

The Supreme Judicial Court of Massachusetts decided that a religious organization can fire a homosexual if the termination has a religious or theological rationale.[7] The *Christian Science Monitor* newspaper fired a lesbian employee because of the Christian Science Church's moral reprobation of homosexuality. The court held that it could not question religious doctrine or belief and would defer to the church in such ecclesiastical matters.

Courts normally defer to religious organizations in matters of hiring, firing, and disciplining their workers in clearly theological matters. If theological issues are not at the core of the church's alleged discrimination, the religious organization can be liable for employment discrimination based on race, sex, creed, ethnic background, and age.

Do the federal labor laws distinguish between religious teachers, ministers, and other church workers such as office personnel?

When religious institutions hire nonordained (or lay) persons, courts analyze their job descriptions for any theological duties. The Supreme Court addressed this issue when a Mormon institution fired a janitor who allegedly failed to observe the church's moral standards.[8] The court stated that a janitor job is a position associated closely enough with the theological mission of the church to come within the exemption that allows it to discriminate when it is carrying out its religious purposes.

Courts have determined that various lay employees do not come within the religious exemption from antidiscrimination laws. A Roman Catholic elementary school fired a lay teacher. The teacher filed suit for age discrimination, and the school claimed that the investigation for discrimination would interfere with its freedom of religion.[9] The Wisconsin Court of Appeals found no "objective measure of the employer's religious requirement."[10] In other words, the court found that the school did not sufficiently state a *theological* reason to shield it from court review. It would appear then that when a lay employee is involved, the court will demand a more detailed explanation of why the firing should be protected as a religious decision.

Consistent with the notion that courts must find some theological reason to exempt employees from the usual antidiscrimination laws, a District of Columbia circuit court held that a Roman Catholic nun could not sue Catholic University of America for sex discrimination and retaliatory conduct.[11] The nun sued after she was denied tenure in the department of canon law. The appeals court stated that such a suit, under Title VII of the Civil Rights Act, would impermissibly involve the court in matters of ecclesiastical polity and policy.

Additionally the Fifth Circuit Court of Appeals dismissed a suit by a female United Methodist minister when she sued her denomination's conference, alleging that the church discriminated against her as a pregnant woman. She claimed that her church denied her maternity benefits and that her salary was disparate compared to her male counterparts. The Fifth Circuit ruled that the Free Exercise Clause, which prohibits the government from interfering with the right to freely exercise religious beliefs, precluded it from hearing the case.[12]

What is sexual harassment and how can it be prevented?

The federal government defines sexual harassment as unwanted and unwelcomed sexual advances, submission to which is an implicit or explicit condition for employment or advancement.[13] Sexual harassment also includes sexual conduct that interferes with a person's performance or creates an offensive and intimidating work environment. Courts considering sexual harassment in religious institutions find no bar to enforcing such federal or state laws.[14] The free expression of religion does not include sexual harassment.

Determining what specific conduct constitutes sexual harassment has proved more difficult, and different courts have arrived at inconsistent, even seemingly contradictory, results. For example, one court ruled that sexual remarks, jokes, and pornographic displays created a hostile work environment, while another court ruled that a manager's remarks that his secretary should perform oral sex for customers and hang a red light over her desk were not sexual harassment.[15] This does not mean, however, that there are no standards for determining sexual harassment.

The standard for defining sexual harassment is the "reasonable victim" standard. Judges or juries must place themselves in the position of the alleged victim in determining whether he or she was offended, intimidated, or thought sexual favors were an explicit or implicit condition of employment or promotion.

Charges of sexual harassment, particularly for religious institutions, are costly. The cost to the institution's reputation must be counted along with the cost of defending the suit. Moreover, if a suit were lost, the religious organization could incur a substantial fine. Every effort should be made by all types of religious institutions (religious schools, places of worship, day-care centers, community service centers, commercial enterprises, and so on) to prevent sexual harassment.

The first step in prevention is to establish a written policy defining and prohibiting sexual misconduct of all kinds and outlining the institutional response. The institutional response should spell out the processes of investigating alleged harassment, adjudicating a harassment case, and punishing proven harassment.

The second step is publicizing, discussing, and enforcing such a policy. This second step involves training workers through seminars, continuing education experiences, in-service training, and other educational opportunities.

Can the religious organization be held liable if it sponsors a dance and one of the youngsters is molested by an employee?

The organization may be held liable for the alleged wrongdoing by its employee under the doctrine of *respondeat superior.* In one case, a mother brought suit against a church when an employee abused her child while the mother attended worship services. The Supreme Court of Alaska, reversing a lower court's decision in favor of the church, ruled that the church would be required to select an employee whose skills were commensurate with the nature of the job.[16] The court stated that the church had to exercise a relatively high standard of care in employing child-care workers. The fact that the church did not interview the alleged perpetrator nor conduct a background check of her could not, as a matter of law, satisfy that standard of care.

In response to allegations of child molestation, a full investigation by the religious organization should be conducted at once. Additionally, full and complete cooperation should be offered to the police and other investigating bodies. Any policies that pertain to alleged employee wrongdoing should be followed in a strict and timely manner. Where administrative decisions are made that either contradict or supplement stated procedures, the circumstances and the rationale that animated such decisions should be carefully noted. Supervisory and management personnel may be called on to justify their decisions either in court or by sworn testimony.

The religious organization should address questions from the press straightforwardly and efficiently. Management and supervisors should not speculate about what happened or assess blame—this should be left to the police and the courts. They should be open and as honest as possible about all the facts at their disposal. A swift and confident administrative approach to a crisis helps to preserve the public trust in the religious organization. Unclear answers and untimely, lethargic investigations can leave the impression that the organization has something to hide, is incompetent, or is unwilling to protect the public.

What is the proper response of the religious institution to rumors or allegations that one of its employees is behaving unethically or immorally?

Rumors and allegations must be investigated in a timely and thorough manner. The religious organization should read anonymous letters and take anonymous phone calls seriously. Investigations are necessary to protect potential victims, the reputation of the alleged perpetrator, and the integrity of the organization. Both the person accused and the person making the allegation should be informed about how the allegations will be investigated, the progress of the investigation, how an administrative hearing will be convened and conducted, what standard of proof will be used for finding fault, and how the alleged victim and alleged perpetrator will be treated in the event that innocence or fault is found through the administrative proceedings.

CHAPTER 9

Contracts

Lex nun cogit ad impossibilia.
The law does not compel a man to do that which he
   cannot possibly perform.

—R. H. Kersley
Broom's Legal Maxims

THE LAW WILL NOT compel someone to do an impossible or futile act; nonetheless, aside from some narrow exceptions, a contract is binding on the parties. Thus the problems in the following hypothetical situation will be obvious.

A religious group wants to hire a leader to conduct its services. The group is reluctant to write a formal contract for the leader's duties. The new leader verbally accepts employment with the promise that she will be paid every two weeks. One month goes by, and she has not been paid. The organization says that she will be paid as soon as the treasurer returns from his European vacation.

Contracts have often been eschewed by religious organizations. It is sometimes assumed that people in religious institutions are honest, and thus contracts are not needed. The making of a contract is seen as an admission of mistrust or as "despiritualizing" the religious work. In reality, contracts simply memorialize and flesh out agreements.

There are two types of contracts: "express" contracts, which are explicitly made, and "implied" contracts, which are made by the actions of the parties.[1] Thus both words and actions can be construed to make a legally cognizable contract.

Three principal elements constitute a proper contract. These elements include an offer, acceptance, and consideration or incentive. An offer is the proposal to do or refrain from doing something in order to secure a benefit. Acceptance is the willingness to agree to such a bargain. The contract must involve a *mutuality* of obligations and benefits. Consideration means that each party gives up something to obtain something in return.

A controversial case that illustrates an *implied* contract is the "palimony" case involving actor Lee Marvin.[2] The facts indicate that Marvin entered into an oral contract with a woman whereby she would forgo her career to conduct domestic work for Marvin and would jointly share his income. The California court ruled that the parties had created a binding contract— regardless of their marital status. Each agreed to take on specific obligations for some benefits.

Can *verbal* agreements be enforced?

As the Marvin case demonstrated, an oral agreement can be construed as an enforceable contract. If the verbal agreement meets the requirements for all contracts, that is, offer, acceptance, and consideration, a verbal agreement will constitute a valid contract.

Verbal agreements, however, lend themselves to their own set of difficulties. They are subject to mismatched memories and general forgetfulness. Oral agreements, however, can be memorialized in several ways. The minutes of a meeting can become evidence of a contract.

Oral agreements are most commonly used in employment matters. In an informal survey among master of divinity students, the respondents revealed that a wide majority who worked for churches had only oral employment agreements. The specific particulars of oral agreements are hard to prove, and they can cause more problems than they alleviate.

Reverend Minker, a sixty-three-year-old Methodist minister, claimed that his bishop assured him that he would be moved to a congregation more suited to his skills, training, and income level. After four years of repeated requests for a new parish, Minker filed suit in federal district court, claiming that he was unlawfully denied a promotion solely because of his age. Among other things he claimed breach of contract. The trial court dismissed the suit, and Minker appealed.[3]

The appeals court remanded the issue of the oral contract to the trial court for further fact finding. The appeals court first found that churches can legally bind themselves by contract—even oral contracts. The court decided that Minker should be allowed to prove that an oral contract existed and that the bishop breached the contract. Minker could present evidence that his bishop made an oral promise to give Minker a more suitable congregation, that Minker gave the bishop some "consideration" for that promise, and that such congregations became available and were not offered to Minker. Minker would also have to prove, however, that review of his evidence would not result in excessive entanglement between the court and the religious organization.

Will the courts normally adjudicate a contract dispute when a religious leader is involved?

If the salary agreement is a legal contract, the religious leader may sue his or her employer for the correct salary payment. The specific types of damages that can be awarded in such a dispute are varied. *Compensatory* damages replace any salary unlawfully withheld. *Liquidated* damages are damages agreed to in advance by the parties in the event the contract is breached. These damages represent the fixed amount of money that the aggrieved party will receive. *Punitive* damages are assessed against the defendant to deter him or her and others from similar future actions. Punitive damages, the amount of which is sometimes left to the discretion of the jury, can be considerable. For example, the plaintiff in the McElroy case, discussed below, claimed compensatory and punitive damages for breach of contract in the amount of $2.5 million.

The major factor in *any* contractual dispute with a religious organization is under what circumstances courts can constitutionally involve themselves in religious disputes. The First Amendment prohibits "excessive entanglement" between government and religious bodies. The following cases illustrate the narrow, constitutional path that courts have taken.

In the Minker case, described above, Minker also sued on the basis of age discrimination under the federal Age Discrimination in Employment Act and its analogous Maryland statute. The federal appeals court, however, dismissed Minker's age discrimination claim on the basis of the First Amendment. A court inquiry would impermissibly entangle government in religious doctrine. Whether the church or its officers followed its denominational polity in assigning pastorates and whether the bishop impermissibly distributed pastorates in favor of young clergy had to be decided by the ecclesiastical authorities themselves. Thus the court will not assess whether one pastor is more fit than another, which it would have to do in a discrimination case. Instead the court focused on the contract issue, which could conceivably be decided without contravention of the First Amendment.

A Georgia appeals court reached a similar result in *McDonnell v. Episcopal Diocese*.[4] When Father McDonnell was relieved of pastoring two mission churches after two years, he sued his diocese for breach of contract. McDonnell claimed that his minimum tenure should have been three years according to a document titled "Diocesan Mission Clergy." He asserted that the document itself was in fact a contract.

The court ruled that it had no jurisdiction over McDonnell's termination. The court was precluded from this inquiry, once again, by the First Amendment's prohibition against government interference with religion. Whether the document was binding, the meaning intended by such a document, and what circumstances warranted a pastor's removal were all ecclesiastical concerns that precluded examination by the court.

In *McElroy v. Guilfoyle* (1990) a priest sued for breach of contract when his bishop refused to pay the priest's legal defense fees. The priest was convicted of sexual offenses involving a minor. The priest claimed that Bishop Guilfoyle, acting with authority to bind the diocese, promised to pay McElroy's legal costs, including attorney's fees.

The court ruled that deciding such an issue would necessitate "detailed exploration" of Roman Catholic canon law, polity, and disposition of priestly functions.[5] This exploration would impermissibly involve court review of the correct ecclesiastical matters, including church practice and governance. Courts are extremely reluctant to impose their authority on strictly religious matters. Thus the court granted the motion made by the diocese and the bishop to dismiss the suit.

Are there some instances in which a court is more likely to resolve a religious dispute?

Courts can refuse to enforce or can void a contract between religious parties. Courts will get more involved if one of the parties to the contract alleges fraud or undue influence. Under such circumstances the complaining party can sue for recision, that is, to have the contract revoked.

A party to a contract cannot intentionally deceive the other party about a fundamental element of the contract without making the contract vulnerable to a claim of fraud. One such case involved a church that bought land under another's name. The church did not reveal to the seller of the property the buyer's real identity. The Euclid congregation, which was duly chartered in Ohio as a not-for-profit corporation, tried to buy land to build a church (a "Kingdom Hall") and signed an initial contract to do so.[6] The neighbors brought pressure to bear on the seller and city officials, and the seller repudiated the contract and sold the land to another buyer.

Determined not to repeat this experience, the Euclid congregation bought land in the name of its president; the president would transfer the land to the church after the deal was done. Subsequently the buyers disclosed who they were and started making plans to build the Kingdom Hall. The court ruled that ordinarily the defrauded seller would have a right to rescind the contract. However, because the buyer subsequently disclosed its true identity, and in this particular case the seller seemed to accept the contract, the seller could not later rescind the contract.

In a case involving undue influence, the court examined the influence of a priest on an infirm woman's last bequest.[7] Mrs. Ross, who was dying, executed a trust under the control of her priest and spiritual advisor, Reverend Conway, a few days before her death. The relatives brought suit to nullify the bequest because of "undue influence." Courts generally are suspicious of persons in close, confidential relationships in which the authority figure gains from the other. Physicians and their patients, lawyers and their clients, and clergy and their congregants fall into this category. Such suspicion can be mollified if disinterested third parties are consulted.[8] Such a third party could include a neutral person who is disassociated from the parties and has no potential for personal gain in this context.

In the Conway case no such neutral person was consulted. In fact the lawyer who drew up the trust was recommended by Conway himself. The court concluded that "the influence which the spiritual advisor of one who is about to die has over such person is one of the most powerful that can be exercised upon the human mind."[9] The court voided the trust.

Courts will examine the role of and benefit to clergy in the affairs of the dying (or people in other crises). Courts will examine contracts benefiting clergy or charities connected with particular clergy. Should a parishioner or spiritual advisee donate or bequeath money or real or tangible property to the religious professional, an independent third party totally unrelated to the contracting parties should be consulted.

What items generally should be included in a comprehensive clergy contract?

Some denominations have minimum compensation standards for their clergy. When this is the case much of the salary and benefit package is predetermined by category and percent. For example, some denominations specify a minimum salary, minimum vacation time, housing allowance, minimum study leave, FICA, and calculate a percentage for pension and health care from the total income. Other denominations do not set such standards. Even where minimum salary and benefits are established, it is suggested that religious professionals consider the following guidance concerning employment contracts.

First, the religious organization should put all agreements in writing. Often verbal agreements are made during the interviewing stage. Sometimes only the main elements (compensation, medical insurance, and vacation time) of employment contracts are discussed. A contract should include the following: when the pastor will begin; when or for what reasons the job will terminate; specified duties; when or how often the salary will be paid; vacation allotment and whether it can be saved or not; disability benefits; life insurance benefits; health insurance for the pastor and dependents; notice required to end the contract; housing allowance; mileage reimbursement or the terms by which a car will be provided; provision for continuing education fees, book allowance, and professional dues; educational leave; clothing allowance; sick leave; provision of malpractice insurance; provision of moving expenses; retirement benefits; percent of time that the minister will be expected to preach; tax responsibilities (who is paying Social Security, Medicaid, etc., and how much); how salary increases will be determined; how often salary will be reassessed; whether the salary will automatically include a cost-of-living adjustment each year; how the church looks upon honoraria and whether there are duties for which the pastor may charge a fee; and any special accommodations such as new office equipment or manse amenities. Any provisions regarding a loan repayment should include specifics such as when payments will be paid, the amount of installments, and the duration of the repayment schedule. Even "small" agreements should be in writing because verbal agreements are easily forgotten over time and different people have different recollections of the same discussion.

An addendum to the contract can be helpful in recording agreements when things need to be added or clarified at a later time. The religious professional should insist that all members of the governing body be fully apprised of all agreements and fully assent to all elements of the agreement. Governing body members who do not have the opportunity to express doubts and opposition to parts of the employment agreement during the negotiating process may be tempted to express disagreement later.

Additionally the religious professional should consider making open and frank disclosures to the hiring committee. The religious candidate with impending separation, divorce, custody hearings, credit trouble, and other such concerns may avoid future allegations of hiding personal information. Of course this is a personal decision, but if disclosure is done and duly recorded by the interview committee, later questions can be defused.

The clergyperson may have to remind the governing board that they should work under the specific terms of their own secular contracts. Efficient management favors written contracts—even for churches. Honesty is not the issue on either part; the issue is keeping agreements orderly and open.

The religious organization and the religious leader should retain easily accessible copies of the contract. They should keep copies of important decisions contained in meeting minutes or in other documents, records of professional expenditures, and other financial records in places where they can be readily reached. Moreover, the documents should be accurately updated.

CHAPTER 10

Agency

Assignatus utitur jute auctoris.
An assignee is clothed with the rights of his
    principal.

—R. H. Kersley
Broom's Legal Maxims

AGENCY IS THE LAW that defines the rights and obligations of agents and their principals. Agents work on behalf of principals. Principals designate agents to work on their behalf. It is not always clear when a religious leader or religious volunteer has the rights of the principal, as the following example illustrates.

Rev. Jones, the new minister, has just started and has arrived at the office. She is anxious to begin working on her first sermon in her new parish. She discovers, however, that her office's computer monitor is broken. The minister's secretary says that he can order one and have it delivered the next day. The secretary says that the governing board told him to "feel free to purchase any office supplies that the new minister may need." When the bill arrives, the church board is astounded, refuses to pay it, and instructs the treasurer to deduct the amount from the minister's educational allowance.

Agency law governs the relationships between people where one conducts business on behalf of the other. Laws govern all aspects of the agency relationship, including the differences between an agent and the principal, how a person becomes an agent, and the legal duties of a principal and an agent.

Officers of religious institutions, staff personnel, and religious professionals may act as agents during the course of their official duties. Every time office supplies are ordered or office machinery is purchased, *someone* acts as an agent. It is important to know the limitations and the liabilities of an agent. Additionally, agents from companies and other institutions do business with religious institutions and such dealings involve legal risk. Minimizing these risks requires an understanding of the legal issues involved in agency relations.

Agents consent to act on another's behalf and to accept the duties and responsibilities inherent in conducting business on another's behalf. Principals consent to have agents conduct business on their behalf and accept the consequences, within limits, of the agent's acts. Usually an agent becomes an agent through authority conferred on him or her by the principal. The authority of the agent is an issue of vital concern for all involved.

The agent's authority to conduct the principal's business may be *actual* (express) or *apparent*.[1] With actual (or "real") authority, a written agreement is the norm. Actual authority, however, can be conferred when both the agent and the principal agree to conduct themselves as agent and principal and accept these respective responsibilities. Sometimes that agreement is written, and sometimes it is simply verbal.

The agent's authority may also be "incidental," that is, incident to express authority. For example, a clergyperson's authority to use the religious organization's car may be incident to an express agreement that the clergyperson visit the sick or attend meetings. In order to assist the clergy in conducting his or her official duties, the principal may also provide the agent with the use of other property such as phones, secretary time, computers, fax machines, photocopy machines, and so on. Clergy should obtain express permission from the religious institution's governing body to use such property when not conducting church business.

With *apparent* authority the agent's authority to conduct the principal's business can be described as "a natural consequence of the express authority granted" to the agent.[2] This authority is implied by the nature of the business and the nature of the express authority. Apparent authority is the authority for the agent to do what is normal or customary business practice even if such authority is not express authority.

The definitions of apparent and incidental authority are considerably blurred. It may help to consider that all the business decisions of an agent cannot be reduced to writing. Emergencies arise; unforeseen events or opportunities occur that require an agent's immediate decision. Incidental or apparent authority is the power to act (or refuse to act) that flows from the purpose and the intention of the principal in giving the agent authority. The agent can use incidental or apparent authority to further the principal's legitimate goals.

When a religious organization hires a head of staff, senior minister, or chief rabbi, the principal-agent rights and responsibilities should be clearly understood. For example, the head of staff's authority to fire and hire employees should be explicit if that is part of the job description. Additionally, the conditions under which the hiring and firing take place should be clear. If the head of staff can order new office supplies, spending limits or conditions should be specified.

Religious organizations should very clearly set the parameters of agents working on their behalf. Their agents should know exactly what is expected of them and have those expectations committed to writing. The principal should consider the circumstances and opportunities that may arise. A religious organization should never acquiesce to an agent's unauthorized use of his or her position. Unauthorized use of an agent's authority can place the church organization, as principal, in a position to pay debts it never intended to incur.

When the church is dealing with an agent from a business or from another organization, it should discuss the scope of this agent's authority prior to making any decisions. The church should know beforehand the limits of the agent's authority. If it seems that an agent is acting beyond his or her authority, the church should contact the agent's principal to clarify or rectify any questions or concerns.

The obligation of the principal in this context is to pay any financial obligation incurred by the agent on behalf of the principal. The agent's obligation to the principal is called a "fiduciary duty." A fiduciary duty necessitates that the agent act in the principal's best interest, to place the principal's interests first, and to act with loyalty toward the principal. An agent is also under the duty to fully identify his or her principal.

An agent's insufficient disclosure of the principal's existence and identity can create liability on the part of the agent.[3] In the *Benjamin Plumbing, Inc., v. Barnet* case, William Whitcomb contracted with the Benjamin Plumbing Company for building work. On letterhead stationery, requesting a bid, Whitcomb signed with the words "for Response for Hunger Network (RHN)." The letterhead was that of the "National Council of Churches in the United States of America, CHURCH WORLD SERVICE." Whitcomb was listed as its regional director. In a subsequent letter accepting the bid, Whitcomb used letterhead stationery with the RHN caption.

The plumbing company completed the work and did not get paid the agreed-upon amount. It brought suit in Wisconsin against Whitcomb, two other members of RHN, and RHN as an unincorporated association. Whitcomb and the other defendants claimed that they were statutorily immune from suit. Wisconsin shields corporate officers from liability under certain circumstances.

The court ruled that Whitcomb was liable for the unpaid amount of $5,600 because although he acted as an agent for RHN he did not fully disclose the corporate status of his principal. This is important because the plumbing company reasonably thought that Whitcomb was personally liable as a contracting party for an unincorporated charitable corporation pursuant to Wisconsin law. Whitcomb was required to fully disclose that RHN was a *corporation*. The court concluded that the plumbing company did not have an affirmative obligation to investigate RHN's corporate status.

The court distinguished between *directors* and *other corporate officers* and *agents* of the corporation. The court found that Wisconsin corporate law provided immunities for corporate officers but not when they acted as agents of undisclosed corporations. Whitcomb was held liable as a party to the plumbing contract and was partially responsible for the payments to the plumbers.

The lesson of this case is that agents acting on behalf of religious organizations need to fully disclose that they are agents. Second, they need to fully disclose exactly for whom they are working. When agents sign documents, they should include their titles indicating that they are signing on behalf of the religious organization.

If a purported church agent enters into a contract without the principal's authorization, may the church disavow the transaction?

A Massachusetts appeals court ruled that a Roman Catholic nun did not have the authority to act as an agent binding her organization.[4] The religious order owned two parcels of land in Boston. The plaintiff, Bisceglia, wanted to buy land from the order. He made a written offer to purchase the land accompanied by $1,000.

The offer was accepted. Papers of purchase and transfer were presented for the order's signature. Sister Bogumilla signed on behalf of her order without making any reference to her representative or official capacity. In fact she was the secretary and a member of the board of directors for her order. When the order refused to execute the transfer, the potential purchaser brought suit to enforce the conveyance. The court found that there was no vote authorizing such a sale. The court also found that, under the order's own constitution, such a sale would require numerous authorizations. No other officer in the order, however, was aware of the sale.

The authorization of officers to act as agents is subject both to state law and to the constitution of the organization itself. In the Bisceglia case, the court found that Massachusetts law does not allow a treasurer to act as an agent in the sale of property—particularly in the case of a charitable organization whose main purpose is strictly religious activities. If the primary and routine purpose of the organization were real estate sales, the outcome may have been different.

Additionally, the court ruled that Sister Bogumilla did not have *apparent* authority to act as an agent in the sale of the property. The order's constitution stated that its purposes were to perfect God's love, to provide health-care services, to provide Christian education, and to minister to contemporary society. Not even under the most liberal theology could such purposes be construed to include routine land sales. Thus the court ruled that Sister Bogumilla's acts could not be construed as those taken pursuant to express, incidental, or apparent authority.

If the religious leader buys a new computer for the religious organization on the direction of the treasurer, but later the governing board refuses to pay for it, who will be responsible for the bill?

The religious leader acts as an agent for the religious organization in making the purchase. The religious organization is the principal because it has authorized another person to act on its behalf. The issue is who is liable when a purported "agent" does not have authority to act (make purchases) on the part of the principal.

If the treasurer had the authority to authorize the pastor to purchase a new computer, then the pastor cannot be held personally responsible for the bill. The governing board probably has to pay for the computer whether it likes it or not.

If the treasurer, on the other hand, had no authority, express or apparent, to buy the computer him- or herself or to confer such authority on the pastor, the treasurer or the pastor may be responsible for the purchase price. The church board with authority to spend money always has the right to ratify, after the fact, an unauthorized act by an agent if it so desires.

Is the unpaid volunteer an agent of the religious institution?

For purposes of *respondent superior*, unpaid volunteers are considered agents in some states. Thus the church can be held liable for the actions of its volunteers if their behavior is foreseeable and within the general ambit of their volunteer duties.[5] In other states courts will look at the degree of control that the charitable organization has over the activities of the volunteer.[6] To answer the question of control, the court in *Doe v. Roman Catholic Church for the Archdiocese* suggested an inquiry into three areas: (1) the degree to which the charity orders the volunteer to perform specific actions; (2) the degree of contact between the charity and the volunteer; and (3) the structural hierarchy of the charity. If the court finds that the volunteer's acts are controlled by the church, then the church will be considered the principal that is responsible for the agent's acts.

What are some "rules of thumb" in addressing agency-principal issues?

The first priority in this arena is to protect the church body from acts of its agents that the agents are unauthorized to do. Obviously with apparent and incidental authority this area of authorization quickly can become subject to dispute. The second priority is to protect the church from people holding themselves out as agents of the church when they are not the church's agents and should not be conducting business for the church. Finally, the church needs protection when dealing with agents of other organizations. The church must be careful not to enter into contracts with people who are not true agents of the principal or conversely are agents of undisclosed principals. Furthermore, the church must be careful that the agent it is dealing with is acting pursuant to express authority to conduct the business in question.

The church should examine its constitution and bylaws with respect to agency and principal issues. For example, do the church bylaws place a dollar limit on the church secretary's authority to purchase office supplies? If no such provisions are set forth, the organization should undertake to study and to draft appropriate provisions promptly.

The religious organization should publicize the rules established in the constitution and bylaws. Even if there are provisions addressing agency issues, they are undermined if staff and key officers are unaware of them. Regular training on agency rules is the best insurance against confusion and violation of the rules. Such education is particularly valuable where officers regularly rotate their membership on boards.

Finally, the religious organization should make the agency-principal rules as simple, practicable, and as "organization friendly" as possible. Agency rules that are hard to follow, either in theory or in practice, are most likely to be violated. A periodic review of management procedures should include agency rules. For instance, where one person has too much authority to conduct business without proper safeguards both that individual and the organization may be a target for misconduct. Reviewing and, if necessary, updating agency rules is an important management tool for the modern church.

Weddings

> Consensus, non concubirus, facit matrimonium.
> It is the consent of the parties, not their cohabita-
> tion, which constitutes a valid marriage.
> —R. H. Kersley
> *Broom's Legal Maxims*

CONSENT IS ONE OF THE elements of a legally binding marriage. Consent to marriage cannot be obtained by fraud, as in the case where a suitor convinced a woman that she was undergoing a religious ritual converting her to the Hindu faith, when in fact the ceremony was a wedding, and she the bride.[1] Consent cannot be obtained by coercion, as in the case in which a suitor threatened to kill his love and blow up her home if she refused to marry him.[2]

Of all the various legal elements that are required for a valid marriage, the bona fide status of the minister is not one of them. If the "religious leader" performing the marriage is not licensed, certified, or officially recognized by the state to perform weddings, the marriage will normally still be valid. It is the minister's continued practice that is at risk. He or she is subject to punishment by the state. In Virginia, for instance, such a person may be sentenced to a year in jail and fined up to $500.[3]

There is of course some legal discussion of what constitutes a duly recognized minister. One state refused to recognize a self-designated minister in a denomination where all new converts could become instant ministers. The law, however, included a special statute for Quakers (and similar denominations) allowing a wedding to be solemnized by the person and in the manner practiced by the society.

In another instance a humanist counselor of the American Humanist Association (AHA) requested permission from Virginia to be recognized as one who could perform weddings. He stated that the AHA did not use the term "minister" or "ordained" but that all counselors were the equivalent of priests or rabbis in traditional religious organizations. The court refused to give this person the privilege to conduct weddings.

Some of the legal constraints regarding weddings include the fact that the couple must contact the state to obtain a valid license before the wedding is performed. Often couples will ask if they can obtain the license after the wedding. The wedding will not be valid if the couple has failed to obtain a license in advance of the wedding. No actual ceremony is required for a marriage to be legal. The couple need only affirmatively answer the question whether they want to be married.

If all of the required witnesses do not sign the wedding certificate, is the wedding still legal?

No. A wedding is only valid in the eyes of the state if the certificate is signed by the minister who performed the wedding and by the required number of witnesses. It is the pastor's job to see that this certificate is appropriately completed and signed by the proper persons. If the certificate is incomplete or is not returned to the state in a reasonable time period, the marriage will not be recognized by the state and the religious leader may be penalized. In Virginia, for example, the minister will be fined $25.[4]

Would it ever be illegal for a clergyperson to marry a couple?

There are situations in which a state will not allow two individuals to marry for reasons related to age, kinship, disease, and so on. Nonetheless, this is not the clergy's responsibility. This is a responsibility reserved for the clerk's office issuing the marriage license. Therefore it is imperative that the clergy have in his or her possession the state marriage license before the ceremony is performed. The minister should examine the license and determine that the license is still timely. Normally licenses are valid for a short period of time; some have a waiting period before they come into effect.

Few states to date recognize the legality of same-gender marriages, and some states specifically prohibit them. While some denominations have designed services for same-gender marriages, these unions may not receive legal status. Moreover, some denominations have special ceremonies to ritualize divorce. The state does not require any ministerial act to effectuate a legal divorce.

Can a pastor charge a fee for performing a wedding?

The pastor must check his or her local law. In some states a minister is in violation of the law if she or he charges more than a nominal amount.[5] Of course the fees could be split up in such a fashion that the cost of the wedding is free, but the fee for the premarital counseling is $300. If the minister does charge a fee for performing the wedding, this is considered income and must be included in figures for income tax purposes. If the couple gratuitously gives the minister a gift for performing the wedding, this is not income and does not need to be included on one's income tax return.

Which state law governs the requirements for a marriage if the wedding is held in a state different from where the couple currently resides or plans to reside or different from where the minister resides?

The legality of weddings is governed by the law of the state where the wedding is performed. If the wedding is valid in the state where it was performed, it will be valid everywhere even though another state would not recognize it if it had been performed within its boundaries. Therefore if the wedding is to be performed for aesthetic or other reasons in another state, the license must be obtained from the state where the marriage is to be performed, and the religious leader must conform to the requirements of that state.

What would be the religious leader's role in premarital or postmarital legal procedures?

Couples will approach ministers for advice on premarital agreements. A premarital agreement sets forth in advance what property each spouse will be entitled to in the event of divorce, preventing the court from deciding what each party has contributed to the marriage in terms of years, children, money, service to the other, and so on. Thus such an agreement is a gamble, valuing in advance what a person's contribution to the marriage will have been at the time of divorce. Usually such an agreement is drawn up when one party has extensive material assets that he or she does not want to lose ownership of should the marriage end.

Putting aside all ethical and religious concerns about marriage, faith, commitment, and generosity, the best advice the minister could give on this topic is that neither party should enter into or sign such an agreement without the assistance of a lawyer. Often these agreements will be attacked later by one of the parties on the grounds that they did not fully understand the ramifications of the document, were deceived on certain facts, or signed the document under duress or coercion. Such allegations can be minimized at the outset by a good lawyer.

The pastor may be approached regarding "living together agreements." A couple may want to clarify in advance property ownership arrangements upon dissolution of the couple's living together. As a separate issue, the couple may want to set forth the legal arrangements between them in the event that one of them dies. Some states and some corporations are allowing employees to designate the person of his or her choice to be included in the employee's health plan and other benefits normally reserved for bona fide spouses.

When a couple has decided to end its marriage, a religious leader may want to suggest that matters of property division; child custody, visitation and support; and alimony are resolved through mediation. Mediation services are often available through the courts, through the local bar association, or through the phone book. Mutual agreement through mediation is usually more satisfying, more successful, and far superior to results obtained through litigation and a judge who brands one spouse a winner and one a loser.

A minister will have developed many of the skills critical to good mediation through counseling training. Mediation as an alternative means of dispute resolution is recognized more and more by state governments; there is no reason why ministers should not be part of this vanguard.

CHAPTER 12

Wills

Nemo est haeres viventis.
No one can be heir during the life of his ancestor.

—R. H. Kersley
Broom's Legal Maxims

THE PERSON WHO IS "entitled" to inherit property cannot be definitively determined until the death of the one who owns the property. Any number of important factors can and do change up to the point of the owner's death. Because ministers spend a great deal of time with people during their illnesses and final years, they sometimes become an heir, much to the dismay of others who thought of themselves as the sole, rightful heirs.

What is a will and what makes it legally enforceable?

A will is a legal document whereby a property owner lists all of his or her assets and designates in advance how he or she wants this property to be disposed of at death.

Creating a legally enforceable will requires elements similar to those that make a marriage valid. When one makes a will, he or she must be of sound mind. Therefore any mental disability, including undue influence, could be grounds for challenging a will. Additionally a minor does not have the legal capacity to make a will. Thus in some states if a will were written by someone under the age of eighteen, it would not be recognized as legal.

The person writing the will must have the intent to create a will. If a person writes a letter stating that he wants to leave his farm to his daughter, the letter embodies a mere whim or wish and does not constitute a will. Moreover, the owner must state that this intention is for the property to pass to the heir upon her or his death.

There are three types of wills: (1) an attested will; (2) a holographic will; and (3) a soldier's and sailor's will. The first is a formal document signed by the person whose will it is (the testator) and at least two witnesses who are competent. The second is written exclusively in the handwriting of the property owner and signed by the testator. Not all states recognize these. Finally, a soldier's or sailor's will involves personal property. It provides a special exception for military personnel from written formalities; thus it may be oral. Many people change and amend their wills with a second document called a "codicil." Others die "intestate," which simply means they have died without a will.

Can a will be challenged by the natural heirs if an elderly person of the congregation changes his or her will on his or her deathbed to leave a large amount of money to the clergyperson who attended him or her during the final days?

Regarding estate bequests to a minister or a church, one must beware of situations in which those who have a natural claim on the estate accuse the minister of undue influence over the testator. Ministers should not in any way assist in the preparation of a will or be a witness to it if the minister, the minister's family, or the church is a beneficiary of the will. This situation arises most often when the testator is one who is susceptible to persuasion. This may be the case if the person is aged, weak, ill, or has diminished mental capacity.

One factor that a court will consider in reviewing a claim for undue influence will be the personality of the minister. The clergy's character will be examined for traits of domination. Next, the relationship between the minister and the testator will be examined. The court will consider whether they had a confidential relationship and whether the minister exerted power over the testator. Finally, the will giving property to the minister becomes some evidence of wrongdoing on the part of the minister. The court will find a presumption that the minister exerted undue influence over the testator if the testator is considered susceptible, if the testator and the minister have a confidential relationship, and if the will leaves property to the minister.

Just because a person is older or frail does not mean that he or she is susceptible to undue influence. The fact remains that a minister very often will have numerous confidential relationships with older parishioners. This is a function of the pastorate. Nonetheless, this is an area in which a minister should act with considerable caution.

What are some of the pitfalls of which ministers should be aware if they are asked for advice on wills?

It is not unlikely that a parishioner would ask a minister for advice regarding charitable donations in a will. The minister may refer the person to the finance commission of the church or to church literature on the topic. The minister should never suggest or draft any will provision that makes the minister (or friends or family) a beneficiary. The minister should be at all times a disinterested party regarding the contents of a will. A minister must avoid even the appearance of impropriety.

If a person states to the pastor that he or she wants to leave a gift to the pastor in the will, the pastor should tell the congregant to speak to a lawyer. The minister should never recommend any particular lawyer nor should the minister obtain a lawyer for the congregant. The minister should recommend that the congregant also consult with a good friend or family member about the matter. Further discussion of the minister's involvement in the will should cease.

Does a clergyperson have any rights if he or she is told by a person that she or he intends to leave a sum of money to the minister, but when the will is read there is no such provision?

No. A mere promise or even a serious commitment to make a minister a beneficiary in a will is void unless formalized according to the elements listed above. Even when a will is formalized, it is *always* amenable to being changed until the testator dies. Thus a will naming a minister as a beneficiary that is later purposely destroyed by the owner will be void.

May a minister be a witness to a will for a member of the congregation?

Yes. Normally, witnesses sign a clause in the will stating that they are over eighteen years of age, personally know the testator, are not related to him or her by blood or marriage, and are not entitled to any portion of the estate. Witnesses also swear that they saw the testator sign the will, that the testator knew that the document was her or his will, and that the testator was of sound mind, over eighteen, and was not under any undue influence regarding the will.

What is a living will?

A *living will* is a document that specifies medical treatment under two circumstances. First, it may cover situations in which the patient is in a coma and terminally ill. Second, it may cover situations in which the patient is in a coma due to some type of accident but expected to live quite a number of years. In either case the patient is not expected to regain consciousness. In a living will the patient specifies beforehand that in the medical situations mentioned above certain treatments should be withheld.

The Supreme Court has stated that patients have a constitutional right to refuse medical treatment if their wishes were clearly made known before they became comatose. The living will can state that the patient does not want artificial respiration, hydration, intravenous feeding, and so on.[1]

A living will should be distinguished from a power of attorney for health care. The health-care power of attorney gives a designated person the right to make medical decisions for a person while she or he is alive but unable to make such decisions personally, such as the widely publicized case in which a husband had to decide whether to end his wife's life-threatening pregnancy while she was unconscious.

Can a minister recommend that a congregant make a living will?

A minister may want to recommend that a congregant state her or his wishes in a living will, particularly before surgery or a medical operation. In fact many hospitals now require patients, before admission, to create living wills. A living will can be beneficial in that it takes pressure off of the family by placing the hard decisions on the patient. The ethical and moral concerns of the congregant would of course be a matter for the minister and the congregant to discuss.

A minister may be a witness to a living will but only if the minister, the minister's family, and the church are not beneficiaries under the patient's will.

CHAPTER 13

Church Ownership and Possession of Property

Sic utere tuo ut alienum non laedas.
Enjoy your own property in such a manner as not
   to injure that of another person.

—R. H. Kersley
Broom's Legal Maxims

THE KEY WORDS cited above are "your own property." The rightful owner of the church is the most pressing question regarding church property and the most often litigated issue for churches. Mediation and arbitration are the best means of resolving such conflicts. Generally the courts will try to decide church property disputes without resolving underlying doctrinal controversies. This principle extends to church polity and church administration disputes as well. The court will not resolve disputes of an ecclesiastical nature or make ecclesiastical determinations.

Two methods for resolving church disputes have evolved.[1] First, the court may take the "deference approach," which mandates that the court defer the decision to the highest adjudicatory body of a hierarchically governed religious organization. The only decision the court needs to make is whether the church is hierarchically organized. If so, the court defers the issue to the highest adjudicatory body in that hierarchy.

Under this approach the only time that a decision of the highest tribunal might be reviewed would be if the person bringing the suit could establish that the tribunal acted with fraud or collusion.[2]

The second method is the "neutral principles approach." The court uses secular concepts of trust and property law to determine the ownership of church property, ignoring doctrinal disputes.[3] Ritual, liturgy of worship, and tenets of faith must be ignored. The neutral principles approach does not extend to membership, church government, order, or discipline disputes.[4]

Both methods are considered proper, and state courts are allowed to choose between them. At least one state court has decided that where the issue involves the interpretation of documents such as wills, deeds, or articles of incorporation, the neutral principles approach should be used. When the issue involves deciding which of two feuding factions is "the true church" for ecclesiastical purposes, then the deference concept should prevail.[5]

What are some of the factors that the courts review when deciding a church property dispute?

The Supreme Court has evaluated three factors in determining church property disputes.[6] First, it determined whether the deed, the will by which the property was donated, or any other document by which the property was held stated expressly that the property would be devoted to the teaching, support, or spread of a specific form of religious doctrine or belief. If this was clearly spelled out, then the faction most closely following the intent of the deed or will would be the one using the property in a way that most closely honored these wishes.

The second relevant factor was whether the property was held by an autonomous religious congregation that was strictly independent of other ecclesiastical associations and owed no loyalty or obligation concerning church government to any higher authority. Thus a dispute between a local congregation and an alleged governing hierarchy would pivot on whether the local church could establish its independence.

Finally, the Court questioned whether the religious congregation holding the property was a subordinate member of a general church organization in which superior ecclesiastical tribunals held supreme judicatory control over the whole membership of that general organization. If this were true, then the general church organization legally possessed the property. The Court would infer a trust relationship between the local congregation and the national church, and the local church would be deemed to hold the local property for the benefit of the national church.

These three factors would be determined by examining the various documents of the church: deeds, articles of incorporation, the constitution, the bylaws, the charter, minutes of the general assembly, and national church polity papers.[7] The court would consider who owns title to the church, who manages and controls the property, how the money was raised to purchase the property, and the practices of the church.

In *Mount Jezreel Christians without a Home v. Board of Trustees*, members of a church sued the board of trustees in an attempt to prevent it from selling the church property.[8] The court reviewed the incorporation documents and determined that the church was incorporated for the purpose of religious worship and holding services at a certain address. Although the title was vested in the trustees, the property was held in trust for the named uses and purposes only. Bona fide members of the congregation were the beneficiaries of the trust, giving them specific legal rights to the property.

CHAPTER 14

Money

Cujus est dare ejus est disponere.
The bestower of a gift has a right to regulate its
disposal.

—R. H. Kersley
Broom's Legal Maxims

O NE OF THE MOST often asked questions in the church is whether monies given to a church must be used as specified. Only when no conditions are placed on a gift is the church free to spend the money in any manner it chooses. "The bestower of a gift has a right to regulate its disposal" is good legal advice when in doubt. The law on this subject is not uniform or well settled. Every state is different; but as a general rule the donor's intent is binding on the church.

An Arizona couple brought an action in court to recover stock valued at $10,000 that they had donated to their church.[1] The donors had requested that the money be spent to build an annex to the Sunday school. The church wanted to use the money to buy land and refused to return the money. The court ruled that once the church took the stock, there was an implied promise to honor the conditions of the donation. The church was bound to comply with the conditions or return the donation.

When a gift is given for a specific purpose, the donor, if still alive, would have authority to redesignate its purpose. When a donation comes to the church with a specific request about how it will be used, particularly when the sum is large, the church may want to ask the donor immediately about the possibility that circumstances may change.

If the desired purpose has become impossible to fulfill for some reason, there is probably room for flexibility. Nonetheless, the result should be as close as possible to the donor's original intent. To be safe, the church may want to bring a legal action in court for a declaratory judgment, which is a ruling from the court in advance that allows a plaintiff the benefit of the court's legal advice about how to proceed.

In *Morristown Trust Co. v. Protestant Episcopal Church*, a trustee filed suit for a declaratory judgment in which the trust was to be used "for the glory of God" and for support of a specific church in a specified location.[2] The church later moved sixty miles away to another city to meet the needs of an Episcopal congregation in that community after all of the families of the original community had departed. The court applied the doctrine of *cy pres*, which means in this instance that when gifts have been made for charitable purposes that cannot literally be executed, the gift will be administered as nearly as possible to the donor's purpose. Thus the court decided that the trust could be used for the new, relocated church.

The same principles apply when land is involved. The deed may well state the purposes for which the land is to be used and be a matter of public record. In *Board of Trustees of Columbia Rd. Methodist Episcopal Church v. Richardson*, a congregant donated land to the church and placed in the deed that the donation was for the sole purpose of erecting a Methodist church and that the construction was to be completed within a year.[3] The church was able to persuade the donor to amend the deed to omit the time requirement. Sometime thereafter the donor spotted a sign on the donated property that read "For Sale—Excellent business location." The court was sympathetic to the donor.

Similarly, in an unusual case, two silver bowls were given to a church in the early 1700s. Several centuries later the church tried to sell them.[4] One of the items was a baptismal basin, on the bottom of which was a Latin inscription stating that it was dedicated for the purpose of holy baptism. The second item was a communion plate that had come to the church through a member's will wherein the donor stated that money would be left to the church for the use of communion items. The court determined that these items could not be sold to a museum because the donors had specified the purpose for which they were to be used.

Can ministers keep money or gifts for performing church duties?

Legally speaking, when the pastor receives a gratuitous gift, he or she does not have to report it as income and may keep it if the donor has not designated the money or gift for church use. To avoid ethical concerns, however, the pastor may want to discuss these practices with the church board so that there is no misunderstanding regarding gifts, honorariums, and so on. If the pastor charges a fee for performing certain duties, then this money is income for purposes of income tax reporting, and the church board should be informed of the pastor's intent to charge this fee.

Do any church monies, like trust funds, have to be kept in distinct bank accounts?

The pastor should never mingle church trust funds with her or his own account. Similarly, the pastor and church workers should not borrow from nor lend money to the church. This makes the church or the individuals extremely vulnerable to allegations of impropriety. As such, it is good legal advice to avoid even the appearance of impropriety. And the pastor or the treasurer should never knowingly draw checks when the funds are insufficient; such an act is tantamount to criminal fraud.

A religious leader would be wise to request an audit of the religious institution's books before he or she assumes leadership. If an audit has recently been conducted, the prospective leader will want to review this information. Regular audits should be part of the organization's normal practice.

Who is responsible for the debts of the church?

The governing board that has the authority to spend money on behalf of the church is responsible for the debts of the church. This assumes that the board exercised its authority according to proper church procedure and that the purchase was conducted in accordance with the board's direction. A person making purchases or procuring services on behalf of the church must do so only with the prior approval of the authorizing board.

Can overzealous fund-raising tactics subject the church to claims of impropriety?

Yes. In a recent case in Washington, D.C., the court allowed church members to proceed with their claims that the ministers had used undue influence to procure contributions.[5] The members testified that church leaders, a bishop and his two sons, pressured them to borrow money and sell their houses in order to contribute $5,000 apiece to the church building fund. The ministers harassed and humiliated those who did not contribute enough and warned that God would "curse" them, "turn his back on them," and even "kill" them. The ministers even pressured members at home. One member stated that she had turned over her child-support payments, and others testified that they had procured second mortgages. Those who did not contribute sufficiently were singled out by name during church services and endured verbal lashings by deacons and other members.

Nine members brought suit, alleging that the ministers had misrepresented the financial condition of the church and their salaries and had misappropriated funds by spending some of the money raised on a $300,000 house.

The ministers responded that members contributed funds of their own free will and were not induced to do so through false statements. They asserted that the dispute was religious in nature and was barred from court review by the First Amendment. Interestingly enough, the court stated that the concept of undue influence (see chap. 12), which normally is used in connection with testamentary bequests (wills), would be applicable to gifts given while a person is alive. Thus if undue influence could be proven, the court would order that the members' gifts be returned to them. Indeed, the court stated that because these people were still alive, their burden of proof would be less than the proof required in the usual case where a minister is accused after a person's death of exerting undue influence. The members would not even have to prove fraud on the part of the religious leader, only psychological dependency on their part or oppressive and coercive behavior by the minister.

The court then addressed appropriate ministerial conduct in these situations. First, the court stated that fund-raising for international or community concerns such as aid to Somalia or homeless persons is acceptable, particularly when the congregant is hearing the fund-raising attempts as a normal part of the worship service. The religious leader's fund-raising attempts, nonetheless, do not have to be for his or her personal benefit to be subject to allegations of undue influence. The court advised that religious leaders must always show the utmost good faith when they are involved in fund-raising.

In a recent twist to the fund-raising cases, a church was sued for continuing to send fund-raising solicitation letters after the church had been notified that the member had died. The deceased member's wife complained that the church was engaging in fraud and intentional infliction of emotional distress. One solicitation letter stated that the minister had spoken to God about the member's condition but that more contributions were necessary for a miracle.

Incidentally, if a church contributor suspects that funds are not being used according to solicitation promises, he or she should approach the church treasurer and anyone else who may be knowledgeable and accountable. No church should be afraid of such questions, and of course any contributing member has a right to know how the church is spending its money. If the member fails to obtain a satisfactory answer, he or she may contact the state attorney general's office, as was done in *Word of Faith World Outreach Center Church, Inc. v. Morales.*[6]

The Texas attorney general investigated allegations that Rev. and Mrs. Tilton ran the church as a sole proprietorship and had direct access to church funds, that the church falsely represented that it provided financial support to a Haitian orphanage, that the church had sent out vials of holy water purporting to be from the Red Sea that in fact were from Taiwan, and that prayer requests solicited by Rev. Tilton never reached him because they were thrown into the trash by the bank that processed the church's mail and deposited its contributions.

How can the church protect itself from embezzlement?

Unfortunately some people who handle church funds believe that they are free to divert these funds. Indeed, some of these embezzled amounts are sizeable. A system of checks and balances is essential. Regularly spot-check the books, and have an audit every year.

Tax Laws

Summa Ratio est quae pro religione facit.
The best rule is that which advances religion.
                              —R. H. Kersley
                              Broom's Legal Maxims

THE LEGAL MAXIM CITED above has resulted in what is commonly called the doctrine of religious "accommodation." Even though the First Amendment prohibits the government from establishing or promoting religion, it has not prevented a number of special exemptions being extended to the church under the law. The best example of this is the tax-exempt status bestowed on churches. Churches are spared the normal burden of taxation—property or other taxes levied on private, for-profit institutions. But this wide exemption once easily granted to religious organizations is being granted more and more judiciously. The Internal Revenue Service is the agency, under the United States Department of the Treasury, authorized to collect taxes. The authority of the IRS to levy its taxing powers is rooted in the U.S. Constitution:

> The Congress shall have Power To lay and collect Taxes, Duties, Imposts, and Excises, to pay the Debts and provide for the common Defense and general Welfare of the United States.[1]

The power to tax *income* is granted by the Sixteenth Amendment, passed in 1913, which reads:

The Congress shall have power to lay and collect taxes on incomes, from whatever source derived.

The religious exemption from the payment of federal income tax is set forth in the Internal Revenue Code. Organizations that are exempt from taxation are:

organized and operated exclusively for religious, charitable . . . or educational purposes . . . no substantial part of the activities of which is carrying on propaganda, or otherwise attempting, to influence legislation . . . and which does not participate in, or intervene in (including the publishing or distributing of statements), any political campaign on behalf of . . . any candidate for public office.[2]

Two general principles should guide religious organizations that attempt to use the above exemption. First, tax-exemption statutes will be construed, but not unreasonably, in favor of taxation.[3] The exemption will be narrowly interpreted, and taxation of the religious organization will be presumed. The presumption flows from the legitimate government interest in collecting taxes.

Second, the one who claims the exemption has the burden of proving exempt status clearly and convincingly.[4] It is up to the religious organization to prove that it is entitled to the exemption.

Can the religious organization be taxed on commercial enterprises?

Religious organizations can be taxed on their commercial enterprises. The Supreme Court upheld sales and use taxes on retail, including mail-order, sales of religious materials in a suit levied by California against Jimmy Swaggart and his incorporated company, Jimmy Swaggart Ministries.[5] The items included Bibles, study manuals, printed sermons, sermon tapes, religious songbooks, T-shirts, mugs, bowls, replicas of the crown of thorns, replicas of the ark of the covenant, and pen and pencil sets.

The California Board of Equalization assessed a $166,145 tax on the mail-order sales totaling nearly $2 million. The corporation challenged the tax on the grounds that it violated both the free exercise clause and the establishment clause of the First Amendment. First, the Court ruled that the California tax did not violate the free exercise clause because it applied neutrally to all of these types of sales without regard to the status of the buyer or the seller. Moreover, the court found that the dollar amount of the tax burden itself was not so excessive as to financially prohibit the company from spreading its message.

Second, the court was equally convinced that the tax did not offend the establishment clause. Because of the sophisticated, computerized accounting procedures already in place in the California tax departments, the state's calculation of the tax did not foster excessive entanglement of the government in the religious affairs of the company.

The *Swaggart* case closely followed another church tax case in which the court ruled that a Texas sales tax exemption for religious publications violated the First Amendment.[6] In *Texas Monthly, Inc., v. Bullock*, the publisher of a nonreligious magazine that was, as such, ineligible for the exemption, sued the state to recover taxes it had paid on its subscription sales. *Texas Monthly, Inc.*, argued that a state sales-tax exemption for religious publications favored religion in violation of the establishment clause. The court found that the state failed to prove that requiring a religious organization to pay the tax would offend religious beliefs or inhibit religious activity. Therefore, the tax exemption impermissibly sponsored religious faith.

Can the state tax land, parking lots, or thrift shops connected to religious organizations?

To the extent that such properties are held exclusively or primarily for religious purposes, they enjoy tax-exempt status. A Texas court of appeals ruled that parking lots belonging to a church were tax exempt.[7] The lower court had ruled for the county, finding that, according to Texas law, the *actual use* of the parking lots, not the *church's primary purpose for owning the property*, was the governing issue in the case. After finding that the church rented 407 of the 447 parking spaces to a business from 7:30 A.M. to 5:00 P.M. Monday through Friday each week, the court concluded that the actual use of the parking lots was secular. The appellate court, however, found that the land was held for the religious organization's use and stated that a court cannot simply weigh the number of hours that the lot is used for secular purposes against the number of hours that the lot is used for religious purposes.

The Supreme Court of Arkansas denied tax-exempt status to single-family dwellings located on the grounds of a boarding school operated by a religious group.[8] Arkansas tax law required that the property be used "exclusively" for school purposes to receive the exemption. While the association maintained school campus dormitories, a box factory, and a gymnasium, the disputed property was a series of twelve detached single-family housing units. The association contended that the units should be tax exempt.

The units, ruled the court, did not satisfy the "exclusive use" rule required by state law. The court interpreted this rule to mean the *primary* use of the property, not the *secondary* use of the property. After finding that the dwellings were rented for residential use to faculty and staff, that faculty and staff lived in the facilities year-round, that no classes were conducted in the units, and that the housing units competed with other rental property owners in the area, the court concluded that their primary use was not for educational purposes.

A church's rental of property presented another type of state tax consideration in an Illinois case.[9] In order to claim tax exemption, the church had to prove that the renters were a charitable organization. An assessed rental value of the property was $7.00 per square foot, and the church rented the property for $1.11 per square foot.

The issue was whether MoMing, which offered classes in contemporary dance for all age groups, met the state criteria to qualify as a charitable organization. The court recited the sixfold criteria: (1) the charitable benefits are available to an indefinite number of persons; (2) the group has no capital, capital stock, or shareholders; (3) the group's funds are obtained mainly from private and public charity; (4) the charity is dispensed to all who need and who apply for it; (5) the needy are not hindered from obtaining the charity's benefits; and (6) the primary use of the property is for charity.

The court heard testimony that MoMing charged substantially less than enough to meet expenses, that community groups were periodically permitted to freely use its facilities, that students unable to pay were provided with work-study options, and that the primary goal of MoMing was to instruct students in contemporary dance and to present performances to the public. The court ruled that MoMing was a charitable organization and exempted the church's rental property from state tax.

In another case, a church was allowed to keep its state tax-exempt status for an unused parsonage and carport.[10] The church placed its carport and parsonage on the market in 1985 and sold them in 1986. During the time the property was for sale, the church used the property to store church records, pews, hymnals, and the pipe organ and as a place to conduct bake sales.

The state department of revenue sued to collect taxes on the property, claiming it was not used for religious purposes during this time. The court ruled that while tax-exempt status in one year does not guarantee tax exemptions for subsequent years, *temporary* vacancy or disuse does not render the property taxable. It would be impracticable and would lack common sense, stated the court, to tax otherwise exempt property immediately upon its disuse.

Can overt political activity jeopardize a religious organization's tax-exempt status?

The 501(c)(3) nonprofit exemption given to religious organizations by law prohibits political campaigning on behalf of any candidate for public office, whether federal, state, or local. The law provides an absolute prohibition. In addition, the exemption requires that "no substantial" part of the organization's activities is spent on influencing legislation. Religious organizations should be cautious about involving themselves in political activities—particularly campaign activities.

Religious institutions must not devote a substantial amount of time and effort to affecting legislation such that the 501(c)(3) exemption would be violated. "Legislation" is defined as, "action by the Congress, by any State legislature, by any local council or similar governing body, or by the public in a referendum, initiative, constitutional amendment, or similar procedure."[11] This definition includes direct and grassroots lobbying and time spent supporting activities preparatory to the development of a legislative position. The courts have ruled that less than 5 percent of an organization's time and effort is not substantial but that 17 percent of an organization's budget would be. Thus, a rule of thumb might be that an organization should not exceed 15 percent of its budget and time and effort on legislative activities.[12] All relevant facts specific to an organization would be reviewed by the court. The courts have determined that testimony given in response to congressional committee solicitation and distribution of nonpartisan research would not constitute actions taken to influence legislation.[13] The organization may want to order the IRS Exempt Organizations Handbook (IRM 7751).

Can insurance trusts established for employees of religious organizations be taxed by the federal government?

A U.S. Court of Appeals held that a trust providing insurance benefits for employees of a religious organization could be taxed.[14] The employees of the religious organization had no control over the trust, and the trustees were appointed by the association's board of directors. The trust provided life, accidental death and dismemberment, and disability insurance. The court concluded that these insurance benefits did not make the insurance trust a "social welfare organization" for tax-exemption purposes.

Even though the association itself was a tax-exempt organization, stated the court, the trust had a "substantial private, nonexempt purpose of providing insurance in exchange for premiums." Courts will scrutinize the purpose and actual function of trusts in order to determine whether they meet the requirements for religious tax exemptions.

CHAPTER 16

How the Church Can Obtain Additional Assistance

Vigilanribus, non dormientibus, ;uta subveniunt.
The laws assist those who are vigilant, not those
who sleep over their rights.

—R. H. Kersley
Broom's Legal Maxims

THE LAW DOES NOT FAVOR one who is dilatory or lazy about pursuing legal claims. Instead, one is encouraged to react in a timely manner to a legal wrong. While the church may not see its role as encouraging litigation, neither should a church be afraid to use the law to assist it in its mission.

Some believe that Martin Luther King Jr. was a genius at using the law to pursue his religious vision. Church leaders owe it to their congregants to be a reliable referral source regarding legal questions. Many people will turn to church leaders with legal questions, as these problems so often embody ethical and moral concerns. One of the most helpful pieces of advice that religious leaders can give congregants is to procure the services of a lawyer so that they may adequately protect themselves and their rights. Additionally, bar associations and local professionals may offer mediation services as an alternative to litigation.

Who can the church contact if it is having problems with a good or service?

The church may want to contact the local or state better business office or a consumer protection office if the issue involves a defective product or service. As a preventative measure, the church should contact these organizations prior to making a significant purchase as they will advise whether any complaints have been lodged against a particular company in the past. Similarly, when a religious organization enters into contracts for construction services, payment and performance bonds should be considered. Background and reference checks need to be pursued.

Who can the church contact if it has a question regarding tax matters?

The federal Internal Revenue Service and the state counterpart will give free tax assistance and advice; however, there is no substitute for a good tax lawyer. This is particularly true if the lawyer is versed in tax law as it relates to 501(c)(3) nonprofit organizations.

What entity can assist if someone in the congregation is being treated unfairly at work, school, or in obtaining housing?

The Equal Employment Opportunities Commission, the Department of Education, and the Housing and Urban Development Agency are charged with protecting people's rights regarding work, education, and housing. Additionally, many states have departments that mirror these federal agencies. The blue pages in the phone book, which cover local, state, and federal government offices, will help identify agencies that can assist with specific problems. Unfair treatment may materialize in banking matters, admissions policies for private clubs or other organizations, zoning decisions, and so on. Federal or state agencies are charged with investigating unfair treatment and advising the citizen of his or her rights under the law.

What if a member of the congregation has been put in jail?

Obtaining a lawyer as quickly as possible is critical to reducing the time that a person may have to remain in jail. When a person is without financial resources, the public defender's office will provide free representation for criminal matters. Many communities have legal-aid societies that offer free or reduced-fee legal services on both criminal and civil matters. Additionally, there are public interest law groups that offer free or reduced-fee legal services. The state or local bar association will have more specific information.

How can a church choose a good lawyer?

Many states and municipalities offer a lawyer's referral and information service. Several local attorneys may have experience with church-related issues. Lawyers and judges have a good sense of the reputations of lawyers in the vicinity. A church can inquire about the reputation of a certain lawyer or request a recommendation for an appropriate lawyer.

Are there any organizations that might provide free legal assistance to a church?

The American Civil Liberties Union will provide free legal services when it deems a case to be of social significance. A more conservative group, the Christian Legal Society, has chapters in almost every state. Many national denominations have people or divisions working solely on legal issues as they affect churches. The National Council of Churches has an ordained counselor who is the director for religious and civil liberty. The Baptist Joint Committee vigorously litigates matters of separation of church and state. Additionally, there are religious liberty lobbying groups that work to influence legislation to ensure that religious rights are adequately protected by the law. Any of these groups could be contacted if the church found itself in the midst of a controversy that appeared to have far-reaching ramifications.

Regarding more mundane legal matters, some law firms in the church community will have a pro bono practice (services offered without charge) as part of their ongoing activities. A church can contact some of the law firms in the community and ask if they offer these pro bono services. Finally, a church should not be timid about asking lawyers in the congregation for advice on any topic. While their expertise may be far removed from the issues at hand, they will have some solid ideas about the best ways to proceed.

Where can a church lodge its complaints about a particular lawyer?

If a religious institution has a complaint against a lawyer, it should first contact the state bar association, which will normally have an ethics committee, misconduct committee, or a grievance committee. The association will have a process whereby one can lodge complaints about lawyers; it may even conduct free arbitrations for fee disputes and malpractice claims against lawyers. If this avenue does not work to the church's satisfaction, it may consider contacting another lawyer.

What other resources are available?

The authors of this book have published a book entitled *Legal Issues and Religious Counseling* (Louisville, Ky.: Westminster John Knox Press, 1993), which provides legal information on three litigation-prone areas for ministers in their counselling activities: (1) failure to maintain a counselee's confidentiality and situations that require a minister/rabbi to reveal a counselee's confidences; (2) sexual misconduct with a counselee; and (3) the provision of ineffective or destructive counseling and/or the duty to prevent harm perpetrated by the counselee.

Additionally, Michael J. Anthony has authored a book entitled *The Effective Church Board: A Handbook for Mentoring and Training Servant Leaders* (Grand Rapids, Mich.: Baker Books, 1993); Paul Chaffee has written *Accountable Leadership: Resources for Worshipping Communities: A Guide through Legal, Financial, and Ethical Issues Facing Congregations Today* (San Francisco, ChurchCare Pub., 1993); and David R. Pollack has written *Business Management in the Local Church* (Chicago: Moody Press, 1992).

Notes

Chapter 1. Litigation

1. *Black's Law Dictionary* (St. Paul, Minn.: West Publishing, 1990), 934.

2. Ibid., 1489.

3. J. S. Carey, "Clergy in Court," *Case and Comment,* November-December 1988, 1.

4. W. P. Keeton, ed. *Prosser and Keeton on Torts,* 5th ed. (St. Paul, Minn.: West Publishing, 1984), § 133.

5. *American Law Reports* 4th (Rochester, N.Y.: Lawyers Cooperative Publishing, 1983), 517.

6. *Restatement of the Law of Torts Second* (St. Paul, Minn.: American Law Institute, 1979), § 895E.

7. Ibid.

8. *Schultz v. Boy Scouts of Am., Inc.*, 65 N.Y.2d 189, 480 N.E.2d 679, 491 N.Y.S.2d 90 (1985).

9. M. P. Singsen, "Charity Is No Defense: The Impact of the Insurance Crisis on Nonprofit Organizations and an Examination of Alternative Insurance Mechanisms," *University of San Francisco Law Review* 22 (1988): 599.

10. Church Audit Procedures Act, 26 U.S.C. § 7611(a)(1) (1984).

11. Ibid., 26 U.S.C. § 7611(b)(l)(A) & (B).

12. *United States v. Church of Scientology*, 973 F.2d 715 (9th Cir. 1992).

13. J. M. Gannon, "Sanctuary: Constitutional Arguments for Protecting Undocumented Refugees," *Suffolk University Law Review* 20 (1986): 951–52.

14. Ibid.

15. Ibid.

16. T. Brom, "Church Sanctuary for Salvadorans," *California Lawyer*, July 1983, 42–43.

17. Gannon, "Sanctuary," 953.

18. Ibid.

19. Brom, "Church Sanctuary for Salvadorans," 42–43.

20. "Church Keeps Secrets," *National Law Journal*, Nov. 30, 1992, 6.

21. Presbyterian Church v. United States, 870 F.2d 518 (9th Cir. 1989).

Chapter 2. Church Procedures

1. G. Taylor, "Removing a Reverend," *National Law Journal* (August 17, 1992), 55.

2. *Burgess v. Rock Creek Baptist Church*, 734 F. Supp. 30 (D.D.C. 1990).

3. *Karen S. v. Streitferdt*, 172 A.D.2d 440, 568 N.Y.S.2d 946 (1991).

Chapter 3. Government Regulatory Laws

1. *St. Agnes Hosp. v. Riddick*, 748 F. Supp. 319 (D. Md. 1990).

2. *Employment Div., Dep't of Human Resources v. Smith*, 494 U.S. 872 (1990).

3. *Rector, Wardens, & Members of Vestry of St. Bartholomew's Church v. City of New York*, 914 F.2d 348 (2d Cir. 1990).

4. E. C. Richardson, "Applying Historic Preservation Ordinances to Church Property: Protecting the Past and Preserving the Constitution," *North Carolina Law Review* 63 (1985): 404.

5. Ibid.

6. P.L. 106–274 (2000).

7. Marshall J. Breger, et al., *In Good Faith a Dialogue on Government Funding of Faith-based Social Services* (Temple University, Penn.: Feinstein Center for American Jewish History, 2000).

8. *Larkin v. Grendel's Den, Inc.*, 459 U.S. 116 (1982).

9. *Larson v. Valente*, 456 U.S. 228 (1982).

10. *Taylor v. City of Fort Lauderdale*, 583 F. Supp. 514 (S.D. Fla. 1984), *rev'd on other grounds*, 810 F. 2d 1551 (11th Cir. 1987).

11. *Church of Scientology Flag Serv. Org., Inc. v. City of Clearwater*, 2 F.3d 1514 (11th Cir. 1993).

12. *Forest Hills Early Learning Center, Inc. v. Grace Baptist Church*, 846 F.2d 260 (4th Cir. 1988).

13. *Oklahoma ex rel. Roberts v. McDonald*, 787 P.2d 466 (1989).

14. *Salvation Army v. Department of Community Affairs*, 919 F.2d 183 (3d Cir. 1990).

15. *Armory Park Neighborhood Ass'n v. Episcopal Community Serv.*, 148 Ariz. 1, 712 P.2d 914 (1985).

16. Americans with Disabilities Act, 56 C.F.R. § 35554 (1991).

17. Ibid.

18. Ibid.

19. Ibid.

20. Fair Housing Act, 42 U.S.C. § 3601 et seq. (1968).

21. Ibid., 42 U.S.C. § 3607.

22. *Good News Club v. Milford Cent. Sch.*, 533 U.S. 98 (2001).

Chapter 5. Copyright

1. *Webster's Ninth New Collegiate Dictionary* (Springfield, Mass.: Merriam-Webster, 1991).

2. A. Latman, R. Gorman, and J. Ginsburg, *Copyright for the Eighties* (Charlottesville, Va.: Michie, 1985), 1.

3. *Basic Books, Inc. v. Kinko's Graphics Co.*, 758 F. Supp. 1522 (S.D.N.Y. 1991).

4. Ibid.

5. Ibid.

6. *Repp v. Webber*, 132 F.3d 882, 889 (2d Cir. 1997).

7. United Presbyterian Church (U.S.A.), *Rightful Use* (Louisville,

Ky.: United Presbyterian Church [U.S.A.], n.d.).

8. Christian Copyright International, 800.234.2446.

9. *Basic Books, Inc. v. Kinko's Graphics, Corp.*, 758 F. Supp. 1522 (S.D.N.Y. 1991).

Chapter 6. Personal Injury

1. W. P. Keeton, ed. *Prosser and Keeton on Torts* 5th ed. (St. Paul, Minn.: West Publishing, 1984).

2. *Harmotta v. Bender*, 411 Pa. Super. 371, 601 A.2d 837 (1991).

3. *Reider v. City of Spring Lake Park*, 480 N.W.2d 662 (Minn. 1992).

4. Ibid.

5. *Coates v. W. W. Babcock Co.*, 203 Ill. App. 3d 165, 560 N.E.2d 1099 (1990).

6. *Lichtenthal v. St. Mary's Church*, 166 A.D.2d 873, 561 N.Y.S.2d 134 (1990).

7. *Frio v. Superior Court*, 203 Cal. App. 3d 1480, 250 Cal. Rptr. 819 (1988).

8. Wire and Electronic Communications Interception and Interception of Oral Communications Act, 18 U.S.C. § 2510 *et seq.* (1988).

9. *Emerson v. Markle*, 539 N.E.2d 35 (Ind. 1989).

10. *Wash. Rev. Code Ann.* § 9.73.030 (West 1988).

11. *Schmidt v. Bishop*, 779 F. Supp. 321 (S.D.N.Y. 1991).

12. *Hiett v. Lake Barcroft Community Ass'n, Inc.*, 244 Va. 191, 418 S.E.2d 894 (1992).

Chapter 7. Defamation

1. *Redmond v. McCool*, 582 So.2d 262 (La. 1991).

2. *Davis v. Black,* 70 Ohio App. 3d 359, 591 N.E.2d 11 (1991).

3. Ibid., 70 Ohio App. 3d 359, 369, 591 N.E.2d 11, 18 (1991).

4. *Hester v. Barnett*, 723 S.W.2d 544 (Mo. 1987).

5. *Murphy v. Harty*, 238 Or. 228, 393 P.2d 206 (1964).

6. *Snyder v. Evangelical Orthodox Church*, 216 Cal. App. 3d 297, 264 Cal. Rptr. 640 (1989).

7. *Black v. Snyder*, 471 N.W.2d 715 (Minn. 1991).

8. *Klagsbrun v. Va'ad Harabonim of Greater Monsey*, 53 F. Supp 2d 732 (D.N.J. 1999); *Hartwig v. Albertus Magnus Coll.*, 93 F. Supp. 2d 200 (D. Conn. 2000).

9. *St. Luke Evangelical Lutheran Church, Inc. v. Smith*, 318 Md. 337, 568 A.2d 35 (1990).

10. *Church of Scientology v. Minnesota State Medical Ass'n Found.*, 264 N.W.2d 152 (Minn. 1978).

11. Ibid., 156.

12. *Hustler Magazine, Inc. v. Falwell*, 485 U.S. 46 (1988).

13. R. McAllister, "Falwell Ruling: Libel Precedent or an Oddity?" *Richmond Times-Dispatch*, August 10, 1986, B1, B6.

14. *Hustler Magazine, Inc. v. Falwell*, 485 U.S. 46, 57 n.5 (1988).

15. *Hargrow v. Long*, 760 F. Supp. 1 (D.D.C. 1989).

16. *Murphy v. Harty*, 238 Or. 228, 393 P.2d 206 (1964).

17. R. K. Bullis, "Child Abuse Reporting Requirements: Liabilities and Immunities for Clergy," *Journal of Pastoral Care* 440 (1990): 244–48.

18. *Mackintosh v. Carter*, 451 N.W.2d 285 (S.D. 1990).

Chapter 8. Employment and Labor Law

1. *Mrozka v. Archdiocese of St. Paul and Minneapolis*, 482 N.W.2d 806 (Minn. 1992).

2. *Byrd v. Faber*, 57 Ohio St. 3d 56, 565 N.E.2d 584 (1991).

3. *Doe v. Samaritan Counseling Center*, 791 P.2d 344 (Alaska, 1990).

4. *Tony & Susan Alamo Found. v. Secretary of Labor*, 471 U.S. 290 (1985).

5. *Dole v. Shenandoah Baptist Church*, 899 F.2d 1389 (4th Cir. 1990).

6. *Minker v. Baltimore Annual Conference of United Methodist Church*, 894 F.2d 1354 (D.C. Cir. 1990).

7. *Madsen v. Erwin*, 395 Mass. 715, 481 N.E.2d 1160 (1985).

8. *Corporation of the Presiding Bishop of Church of Jesus Christ of Latter-Day Saints v. Amos*, 483 U.S. 327 (1987).

9. *Sacred Heart School Bd. v. Labor & Indus. Review Comm'n*, 157 Wisc. 2d 638, 460 N.W.2d 430 (1990).

10. Ibid., 157 Wisc. 2d 638, 642, 460 N.W.2d 430, 432 (1990).

11. *EEOC v. Catholic Univ. of America*, 83 F.3d 455 (D.C. Cir. 1996).

12. *Combs v. Central Tex. Ann. Conf., United Methodist Church*, 173 F.3d 343 (5th Cir. 1999).

13. *Equal Employment Opportunities Commission (EEOC)*, 29 C.F.R. Pt. 1604 (1980).

14. *Black v. Snyder*, 471 N.W.2d 715 (Minn. 1991).

15. S. B. Goldberg, "Hostile Environments," *ABA Journal* 77 (1991): 90–92.

16. *Broderick v. King's Way Assembly of God Church*, 808 P.2d 1211 (Alaska, 1991).

Chapter 9. Contracts

1. J. Lieberman and G. Siedel, *Business Law and the Legal Environment* (Washington, D.C.: Harcourt, Brace and Jovanovich, 1985).

2. *Marvin v. Marvin*, 18 Cal. 3d 660, 557 P.2d 106, 134 Cal. Rptr. 815 (1976).

3. *Minker v. Baltimore Annual Conference of United Methodist Church*, 894 F.2d 1354 (D.C. Cir. 1990).

4. *McDonnell v. Episcopal Diocese*, 191 Ga. App. 174, 381 S.E.2d 126 (1989).

5. *McElroy v. Guilfoyle*, 247 N.J. Super. 582, 587, 589 A.2d 1082, 1084 (1990).

6. *Keyerleber v. Euclid Congregation of Jehovah's Witnesses*, 103 Ohio App. 423, 143 N.E.2d 313 (1957).

7. *Ross v. Conway*, 92 Cal. 632, 28 P. 785 (1892).

8. C. M. Guidroz, "Use of Non-confidential Relationship Undue Influence in Contract Recision," *Notre Dame Lawyer* 46 (1974): 631–42, 641.

9. *Ross v. Conway*, 92 Cal. 632, 636, 28 P. 785, 786 (1892).

Chapter 10. Agency

1. H. Reuschlein and W. Gregory, *The Law of Agency and Partnership* (St. Paul, Minn.: West Publishing, 1990), 34–38.

2. Ibid., 42.

3. *Benjamin Plumbing, Inc. v. Barnes*, 162 Wis. 2d 837, 470 N.W.2d 888 (1991).

4. *Bisceglia v. Bernadine Sisters of the Third Order of St. Francis*, 29 Mass. App. Ct. 959, 560 N.E.2d 567 (1990).

5. *Cordts v. Boy Scouts of Am., Inc.*, 205 Cal. App. 3d 716, 252 Cal. Rptr. 629 (1988) (ordered not to be officially published).

6. *Doe v. Roman Catholic Church for the Archdiocese*, 602 So.2d 129 (La.), *vacated on other grounds*, 606 So.2d 524 (1992).

Chapter 11. Weddings

1. B. Burnett, ed., *Every Woman's Legal Guide* (Garden City, N.Y.: Doubleday, 1983), 128.

2. Ibid., 129.

3. *Va. Code Ann.* § 20-28 (Michie 1990).

4. Ibid.

5. Ibid.

Chapter 12. Wills

1. *Cruzan by Cruzan v. Director, Mo. Dep't of Health*, 497 U.S. 261 (1990).

Chapter 13. Church Ownership and Possession of Property

1. *St. Cyprian's Chapel, Inc. v. Fraternity of the Apostles of Jesus and Mary*, No. 83-6030, 1985 WL 2877 (E.D. Pa. Sept. 16, 1985), *aff'd*, 800 F.2d 1138 (3d Cir. 1986).

2. *Serbian Eastern Orthodox Diocese for the United States v. Milivojevich*, 426 U.S. 696 (1976).

3. *St. Cyprian's Chappel*, at 6.

4. *Burgess v. Rock Creek Baptist Church*, 734 F. Supp. 30 (D.D.C. 1990).

5. Ibid.

6. *Watson v. Jones*, 80 U.S. 679 (1871).

7. *Southern Ohio State Executive Offices of Church of God v. Fairborn Church of God*, 61 Ohio App. 3d 526, 573 N.E.2d 172 (1990).

8. *Mount Jezreel Christians without a Home v. Board of Trustees*, 582 A.2d 237 (D.C. 1990).

Chapter 14. Money

1. *Dunaway v. First Presbyterian Church*, 103 Ariz. 349, 442 P.2d 93 (1968).

2. *Morristown Trust Co. v. Protestant Episcopal Church*, 1 N.J. Super. 418, 61 A.2d 762 (1948).

3. *Board of Trustees of Columbia Rd. Methodist Episcopal Church v. Richardson*, 216 La. 633, 44 So.2d 321 (1949).

4. *Newhall v. Second Church and Soc'y of Boston*, 349 Mass. 493, 209 N.E.2d 296 (1965).

5. *Roberts-Douglas v. Meares*, 624 A.2d 405 (D.C. App. 1992), *reaff'd as modified*, 624 A.2d 431 (D.C. App. 1993).

6. *Word of Faith World Outreach Center Church, Inc. v. Morales*, 986 F.2d 962 (5th Cir. 1993).

Chapter 15. Tax Laws

1. Article I, § 8 of the U.S. Constitution.

2. Internal Revenue Code, 26 U.S.C. § 501(c)(3) (2002).

3. *Our Savior Lutheran Church v. Department of Revenue*, 204 Ill. App. 3d 1055, 562 N.E.2d 1198 (1990).

4. *Resurrection Lutheran Church v. Department of Revenue*, 212 111. App. 3d 964, 571 N.E.2d 989 (1991).

5. *Jimmy Swaggart Ministries v. Board of Equalization*, 493 U.S. 378 (1990).

6. *Texas Monthly, Inc. v. Bullock*, 489 U.S. 1 (1989).

7. *First Baptist Church v. Bexar County Appraisal Review Bd.*, 833 S.W.2d 108 (Tex. 1992).

8. *Arkansas Conference Ass'n of Seventh Day Adventist, Inc. v. Benton County Bd. of Equalization*, 304 Ark. 95, 800 S.W.2d 426 (1990).

9. *Resurrection Lutheran Church v. Department of Revenue*, 212 Ill. App. 3d 964, 571 N.E.2d 989 (1991).

10. *Our Savior Lutheran Church v. Department of Revenue*, 204 Ill. App. 3d 1055, 562 N.E.2d 1198 (1990).

11. W. R. Caron and D. Dessingue, " I. R. C. § 501(c)(3): Practical and Constitutional Implications of 'Political' Activity Restrictions," *Journal of Law and Politics* 2 (1985): 172.

12. Ibid., 172, n.16.

13. Ibid., 172, 173.

14. *American Ass'n of Christian Schools Voluntary Employees Beneficiary Ass'n Welfare Plan Trust By Janney v. United States*, 850 F.2d 1510 (11th Cir. 1988).

Bibliography

American Law Reports. Rochester, New York: Lawyers Cooperative Publishing Co., 1985.

Anthony, Michael. *The Effective Church Board: A Handbook for Mentoring and Training Servant Leaders*. Grand Rapids, Mich.: Baker Book House, 1993.

Black's Law Dictionary. St. Paul: West Publishing Co., 1999.

Brom, T. "Church Sanctuary for Salvadorans." *California Lawyer*, July 1983, 42–43.

Bullis, R. K. "Child Abuse Reporting Requirements: Liabilities and Immunities for Clergy." *Journal of Pastoral Care* 44.3 (1990): 244–48.

Bullis, R. K., and C. S. Mazur. *Legal Issues and Religious Counseling*. Louisville, Ky.: Westminster/John Knox, 1993.

Burnett, B., ed. *EveryWoman's Legal Guide*. Garden City, N.Y.: Doubleday and Co., 1983.

Carey, J. S. "Clergy in Court." *Case and Comment*, November-December 1988, 1.

Caron, W. R., and D. Dessingue. "I.R.C. § 501(c)(3): Practical and Constitutional Implications of 'Political' Activity Restrictions." *Journal of Law and Politics* 2 (1985): 169–200.

Chaffee, Paul. *Accountable Leadership: Resources for Worshipping Communities—A Guide through Legal, Financial, and Ethical Issues Facing Congregations Today*. San Francisco: ChurchCare Publishing, 1993.

"Church Keeps Secrets." *National Law Journal*, November 30, 1992, 6.

Gannon, J. M. "Sanctuary: Constitutional Arguments for Protecting Undocumented Refugees." *Suffolk University Law Review* 20 (1986): 949–88.

Goldberg, S. B. "Hostile Environments." *ABA Journal* 77 (1991): 90–92.

Guidroz, C. M. "Use of Non-confidential Relationship Undue Influence in Contract Recision." *Notre Dame Lawyer* 46 (1974): 631–42.

Keeton, W. P., ed. *Prosser and Keeton on Torts*. 5th ed. St. Paul, Minn.: West Publishing Co., 1984.

Kersley, R. H. *Broom's Legal Maxims*. 10th ed. London: Sweet and Maxwell, 1939.

Latman, A., R. Gorman, and J. Ginsburg. *Copyright for the Eighties*. Charlottesville, Va.: Michie, 1985.

Lieberman, J., and G. Siedel. *Business Law and the Legal Environment*. Washington, D.C.: Harcourt, Brace and Jovanovich, 1985.

McAllister, R. "Falwell Ruling: Libel Precedent or an Oddity?" *Richmond Times-Dispatch*, August 10, 1986, B1, B6.

McMenamin, R. W. "Civil Interference and Clerical Liability." *The Jurist* 45 (1985): 275–88.

Pollock, David. *Business Management in the Local Church*. Chicago: Moody Press, 1992.

Restatement of the Law of Torts. St. Paul, Minn.: American Law Institute, 1995.

Reuschlein, H., and W. Gregory. *The Law of Agency and Partnership*. St. Paul, Minn.: West Publishing Co., 1990.

Richardson, E. C. "Applying Historic Preservation Ordinances to Church Property: Protecting the Past and Preserving the Constitution." *North Carolina Law Review* 63 (1985): 404.

Taylor, G. "Removing a Reverend." *National Law Journal*, August 17, 1992, 55.

United Presbyterian Church (USA). *Rightful Use*. Louisville, Ky.: United Presbyterian Church (USA), n.d.

Webster's Ninth New Collegiate Dictionary. Springfield, Mass.: Merriam-Webster, 1992.

FUTURING YOUR CHURCH
Finding Your Vision and Making It Work
GEORGE B. THOMPSON JR.

This resource allows church leaders to explore their congregation's heritage, its current context, and its theological bearings. Thompson provides insights that enable church members to discern what God is currently calling the church to do in this time and place. It is a practical, helpful tool for futuring ministry.　　ISBN 0-8298-1331-4/paper/128 pages/$14.95

SO YOU ARE A CHURCH MEMBER
Revised and Updated
ROBERT T. FAUTH

What does it mean to be a church member? What is the responsibility of a church member? These questions and more are addressed in this condensed handbook designed especially for new members of the United Church of Christ and other Protestant denominations.

ISBN 0-8298-1101-X/paper/64 pages/$3.95

YOU BELONG
A Handbook for Church Members
ALLEN H. MARHEINE

This is a practical handbook for the "new or veteran church member who wants to be more than a name on a membership roster." It provides useful insights for a local church member of any denomination.

ISBN 0-8298-1104-4/paper/96 pages/$4.95

To order these or any other books from The Pilgrim Press call or write to:

The Pilgrim Press
700 Prospect Avenue East
Cleveland, Ohio 44115-1100

Phone orders: 800.537.3394
Fax orders: 216.736.2206

Please include shipping charges of $4.00 for the first book and 75¢ for each additional book.

Or order from our Web sites at <www.pilgrimpress.com> and <www.ucpress.com>.

Prices subject to change without notice.